# ENDORSEMENTS

For me, Randy Clark is the most trusted voice in the healing ministry today. Whether we're looking at character, biblical insights, compassion, or faithfulness over time, he continues to lead the charge in each of these realms. While he'd be the first to point to his imperfections, I've worked with him around the world, and I am constantly challenged by his sterling example. His research, both into Scripture and church history, is that of a seasoned scholar. Yet this book is also intensely practical. Reading *Authority to Heal* is like sitting down with Randy, one on one, having the privilege to hear his personal story laced with priceless insights. This book is sure to release grace for the healing ministry to all who read it.

BILL JOHNSON
Author of *When Heaven Invades Earth*
Senior Pastor, Bethel Church
Redding, CA

Randy Clark's heart is to have you move in the same or greater healings and miracles that follow him. As you read about his journey, the same anointing will jump on you! This is a real "how to" book!

SID ROTH
Host, *It's Supernatural!*
*New York Times* best-selling author of
*Heaven Is Beyond Your Wildest Expectations*

Randy Clark is one of my greatest heroes, and God used him to bring radical healing and transformation in my life. Randy walks in such a powerful father anointing; his heart is to impart and teach everything he has learned to the next generation. I pray that God will use his book *Authority to Heal* to teach and train you in healing ministry and encourage you to pray for the sick. God is kind and full of compassion to heal, and healing is a gift for every Christian to walk in, not just for certain people or certain places. Read this book and amp up your journey to heal the sick in the name of Jesus.

HEIDI G. BAKER, PhD
Co-founder and director of Iris Global
Author of *Birthing the Miraculous*

God's desire is to establish His Kingdom—His rule and reign here on earth—as it is in heaven. He invites us to co-labor with Him in touching and transforming lives with His power and love. Until June 6, 1995, I was blinded in a dispensational cessationist worldview. One encounter and impartation changed everything as Randy Clark prayed for me. My eyes were opened! *Authority to Heal* is the textbook that we all need to represent Jesus on earth. *Authority to Heal* will change you and you will then become an agent of change.

LEIF HETLAND
President, Global Mission Awareness
Author of *Seeing Through Heaven's Eyes*

Randy Clark's superb book *Authority to Heal* represents a new standard in books on healing. He combines the most outstanding experience in practical healing ministry with the most thorough, fresh, and penetrating scholarship as he lays out the biblical, theological, and historical analysis of the issues. This book not only tells you about the authority to heal, it shows you—a rare combination.

*Authority to Heal* is a most appropriate title for this work. This "authority," long denied in church tradition, especially in Protestant theology, actually has its roots in the very core of mankind's experience with God.

Adam's mission from God was virtually identical to that of Jesus' disciples: 1) intimacy with God; 2) a task of "naming"—announcing or proclaiming God's creative work; and 3) to take authority over (to "manage" and "guard" God's creation—the "guard" part was unclear until the serpent showed up!).

Mark 3:14-15 is the key source for this same (though this time more successful) mandate. Jesus chose His commissioned ones to: 1) "be with Him"; 2) to proclaim/announce God's re-creative work—the Kingdom of power; and 3) "to take authority to cast out evil spirits" (to tread on serpents). *Authority to Heal*, then, captures and proclaims the very essence of God's central mission to all of us!

After surveying the vast bibliography of works on Christian healing recently produced by J.D. King, I have seen no other work that is the equal of Randy Clark's new book. It is simply the best. This should be the "go to" textbook on healing for seminaries, Bible colleges, and church mission schools.

In His great love,

JON RUTHVEN

Author of *What's Wrong with Protestant Theology? Traditions vs. Biblical Emphasis* and *On the Cessation of the Charismata*

*Authority to Heal* restores the original good news of Jesus Christ by representing the gospel of the Kingdom—a gospel of redeeming forgiveness, power, and authority. Dr. Randy Clark offers the biblical, historical, and theological authentication of the full truth of the gospel in an excellent way. Dr. Clark is a transparent practitioner of healing and a first-rate theologian of instruction. I wholeheartedly recommend pastors, seminarians, church leaders, and theologians to read this extraordinary book that may bring a new Pentecost.

DR. ANDREW PARK
Professor of Theology and Ethics
United Theological Seminary

Whether this planet on which we live lasts another thousand years—which I tend to hold as unlikely, or a few brief years which I honestly believe to be probable—I believe that my spiritual son, Randy Clark, will be viewed as the man whose life, writings, ministry and voice did more to restore the subject of healing to its deserved position in Biblical thinking than any other man in Christian history. He believes the Bible firmly and, to the limit of his intentions and practice, seeks not only to obey it, but boldly articulate its contents.

I love this book for its wide scope, its careful correctness, its thoroughness with precision. I cannot imagine a fairer approach combined with a bolder humility and meeker spirit than are obvious in this work.

However, I do not buy books for their subject or writing style. I obtain them on the basis of my knowledge of the author. I believe firmly in Randy Clark's authenticity, reliability and relevance!

My word to every potential reader: In whatever stream of Christianity you live and move and have your being, do not neglect the words, thoughts and claims of this book and this man who belongs to us all and lives among us for our benefit and God's glory.

He is a man, not only for the century we live in but the age of which we all are a part. We do well to harvest the ripe fruit of his pen and heart.

Well done, Son Randy! This is a message for our time. We gladly receive it!

JACK TAYLOR, President
Dimensions Ministries
Melbourne, Florida

Randy Clark is a delightful gentleman, scholar and healing evangelist with a worldwide ministry. His new book *Authority to Heal* is a wonderful treatment of healing from a Biblical, historical and theological perspective. Added to this are many personal testimonies of healing from his many years of ministry. Based on research from his 2013 Doctor of Ministry dissertation from the United Theological Seminary in Dayton, Ohio, this book will be a welcome and readable source for anyone who wants to gain a more in depth understanding of healing at this time in salvation history.

VINSON SYNAN
Dean Emeritus, Regent University School of Divinity
Author of *Century of the Holy Spirit*

In *Authority to Heal*, Randy Clark demonstrates that he is not only a healing practitioner, he is also a scholar of church history and theology. The book offers insights that will be enlightening not only to religious believers, but also to academics and skeptics who want a clearer understanding of the place of healing in the history of Christianity. The book is unique in that it both chronicles the personal experiences of one of the most influential pentecostal practitioners of healing prayer alive today and also contextualizes this narrative within well-researched theological and historical analysis. This book can serve as a useful introduction to the topic of Christian prayer for healing as well as provide new perspectives for those already well-versed in the subject.

CANDY GUNTHER BROWN
Professor of Religious Studies, Indiana University
Author of *Testing Prayer: Science and Healing*

As a practitioner in healing ministry who also values research regarding the history, understanding and practice of healing ministry, Randy Clark is equipped in a very special way to bridge the wide gap between practitioners and researchers.

Here he not only draws on his long-term experience and synthesis of other sources but also presents fresh research from his own ministry setting.

DR. CRAIG KEENER
Professor of New Testament, Asbury Theological Seminary
Author and compiler of *Miracles: The Credibility of the New Testament Accounts*, *Acts: an Exegetical Commentary*, and *The Mind of the Spirit: Paul's Approach to Transformed Thinking*.

Randy Clark is a remarkable interpreter of God's healing work today. Knowing Randy and reading his books have had a huge impact on my own faith and my understanding of the healing power of the Holy Spirit. In this latest work Randy draws insights from Scripture, church history , and his own experience to teach us about the ministry of healing. I'm grateful for the opportunity to continue to learn from this humble and anointed servant of God.

DAVID F. WATSON, PHD
Academic Dean and Associate Professor of New Testament
United Theological Seminary

# AUTHORITY
## to
# HEAL

RESTORING THE LOST INHERITANCE OF
*God's Healing Power*

## RANDY CLARK

DESTINY IMAGE® PUBLISHERS, INC.

P.O. Box 310, Shippensburg, PA 17257-0310

*"Promoting Inspired Lives."*

This book and all other Destiny Image and Destiny Image Fiction books are available at Christian bookstores and distributors worldwide.

Cover design by Eileen Rockwell
Interior design by Terry Clifton

For more information on foreign distributors, call 717-532-3040.

Reach us on the Internet: www.destinyimage.com.

ISBN 13 TP: 978-0-7684-0876-8
ISBN 13 eBook: 978-0-7684-0877-5

For Worldwide Distribution, Printed in the U.S.A.

1 2 3 4 5 6 7 8 / 20 19 18 17 16

# ACKNOWLEDGMENTS

I wish to thank the following people who have encouraged, enabled, and equipped me to not only complete this book, which was based upon parts of my doctoral thesis, but who have advised or assisted me in the original thesis project, as well as those who helped in the transition from academic thesis to book. I could not have completed this project without their help. The limitations and imperfections of this work are mine alone. However, there would have been more limitations and imperfections without the aid of many of my staff, mentors, and other doctors, professors, and theologians.

I want to thank those who served as my context associates, professional associates, and peer associates. My context associates were Paul Martini, who helped interview, videotape, and record healing statistics while serving as my personal assistant, traveling and ministering with me for the year of this study; Vicki West Henady, who helped with conducting the qualitative interviews, writing field notes, and assisting in the exacting work of citations. Vicki's task was an important one because this thesis was not written from a cubicle at the library or even from an office. Most of it was written on airplanes, in hotel rooms, or at home in bed when my wife, DeAnne, was asleep. In some ways, parts of the thesis were written backward—instead of having books from which research was done, notes were kept with pages for quotes, and much of the work was done from my memory of books read over the years. Then the books had to be researched to find the information mentioned in the thesis. Vicki was a great help in this way as well as helping to edit and format the original thesis. Thank you, Vicki, for all you did in transcribing testimonies, chasing down testimonies, and verifying sources. Thanks for helping to put back into this book the scores of pages of testimonies that could not be part of an academic thesis. Without these stories, the book would not be nearly as interesting or as powerful as it is. In its present form it brings much more glory to God by testifying to what He has done.

I want to thank those on my staff who helped with my thesis, which formed the basis of this book. Marion Hayes was the primary editor who had the challenging job of trying to keep the various versions of my thesis straight. Many e-mail communications occurred as she sent me the latest versions with instructions of what I still needed to do. She would then edit what I had finished. Her eye for detail and editorial work was a lifesaver. Caleb Ostby was an assistant researcher who helped by calling people to follow up on testimonies. Caleb also took on some of Paul Martini's responsibilities when Paul could not be with me. Caleb traveled to several events during the year and interviewed, videotaped, and kept track of our work and helped evaluate some of the data. Canaan Henady was the main person on our team from the Media Production Department at Global who traveled to most of the larger meetings with me, shooting videos and testimonies. I would also like to thank Rebecca Rinker and Christian Imbesi from Global's Media Production Department, as well as my son,

Jeremiah Clark, who helped with footnoting and making sure the citations were correct for earlier versions of the thesis and for helping find citation information.

I want to thank Tom Jones, my peer associate, who is one of the vice presidents of Global Awakening and who travels even more than me. Your friendship has been one of the greatest blessings of my life. Your wisdom has saved my ministry. You gave me back my life by carrying the responsibilities of the several director roles you have had at Global. I do not think I would have enrolled in the Doctor of Ministry program without you, and then this book would never have been written in its present form.

I thank my faculty mentors for all your input into my life, not just this project. Your input was such a great help, and your constructive feedback and editorial advice was crucial to the betterment of my thesis upon which this book is written. I thank you for being willing to be my mentors.

Jon Ruthven and Gary Greig, you were the two professors I had asked God for even before I started this doctoral program at United Theological Seminary. The insights I gained from both of you, and especially Jon, have made a tremendous impact on my understanding of the Kingdom of God, faith, the gospel, and their interrelationship. I feel God gave me the best—my heart's desire. Before I met you in person, I was already indebted to both of you for what I had learned from you through your writings. Gary, your eye for detail is amazing. Your depth of knowledge is amazing. Jon, you are my favorite theologian.

I want to thank my United Theological Seminary faculty mentor, Dr. Andrew Sung Park. Andrew, God used you to bring me to United Theological Seminary. Thank you for recruiting me and for recognizing my potential for theological reflection and practical application. You have been a "Barnabas" to me. I believe God has purposes greater than either of us imagined by connecting us to one another.

I want to thank my professional associates for their input into my life and the thesis upon which this book is based. Martin Moore-Ede, MD, PhD; Stephen Mory, MD, Ph.D; and John Park, MD. Thank you for reading chapters three through five of the thesis and giving me your professional medical advice. Also, thank you for recommending some articles from the medical field. (Sections of the thesis upon which this book is based have been omitted; the sections of the thesis that were more medical than theological have not been incorporated in this book. That information will become part of a later book.)

I want to thank the theologians and religious studies professors who read the chapters dealing with the theoretical basis for physical healing and the biblical, theological, and historical foundations and their integration. Thank you for your much-needed feedback and for sometimes correcting me when I misunderstood something or was unknowingly misrepresenting a movement or part of the Church.

Dr. Mary Healey, thank you for helping me with the areas that dealt with the Catholic Church. You brought a correction to a blind spot in my understanding, especially in regard to Aquinas. Your many insights were very helpful, and I hope you will be able to see how you tempered me and made me a more usable vessel in the Lord's vineyard. I thank God for opening the door to have one of the most significant theologians in the Roman Catholic Church in North America advise me.

Dr. Craig Keener, I am amazed that you took the time to read the long section on the biblical, theological, and historical foundations. Your insights have made that section stronger. Your two-volume book, *Miracles,* was one of the highlights of the reading for the doctoral program. Again, I thank God that in His providence He opened the door to one of the most recognized biblical scholars in North America to give insight and perspective on my writing. Your friendship is important to me, as have been our discussions—even when we didn't always see eye to eye.

Drs. Joshua and Candy Brown, thank you for your encouragement and advice, as well as input. Getting to know you over the years has been a joy in my life. Thank you for inviting me to the symposium, "Healing: Catholic, Protestant, and Medical Perspectives," at St. Louis University. Being part of the lecturers for the symposium was a catalyst God used to light a fire in me for reaching into the medical community. Candy, your books have been a great blessing to many, including me.

Dr. Michael McClymond, thank you for your suggestions and for recommending articles that were helpful to my studies. Thank you for your support and the wisdom you freely offered me when I reached out to you for advice. You are one of the great historical theologians alive today.

Dr. David Zaritsky, thank you for your hospitality, your zeal for the Lord, your input on the international ministry trips, and your professional medical opinions and interpretations. Thank you for your encouraging words and your willingness to help us with the healing verifications.

A special thanks to Larry Sparks, MDiv, Publisher, Destiny Image Publications. You had faith that this could be a book that would bless and encourage pastors, lay people, and also theologians and biblical scholars. You were a great help and played a key role in turning the original thesis into this book. This book would not exist without your input, huge editorial oversight, and suggestions. And thank you to all those at Destiny Image who helped in the production of this book, from editing to cover design to marketing.

I want to thank Susan Thompson for further editorial service, for the addition of material from Bishop John Howe's book *Anointed by the Spirit*, for adding testimonies to the manuscript, and for her extensive work on the study guide. Her editorial expertise has helped mold the manuscript into what it is now.

Thanks to Phill Olson, who also helped with citation work, research, and advice as we neared completion of this manuscript.

Finally, and most importantly, I want to thank my family. Both the thesis and the book have taken more time away from all of you than I anticipated. Each one of you had to forgive me for so often being preoccupied with this thesis, and later for the time I had to put into reviewing the final stages of this book. Thank you, DeAnne, for being willing to give up much of the too little time we have together, and for your understanding and your unwavering support when I was under deadline pressure. Thank you to each of my children and their mates who put up with a preoccupied dad. Josh and Tonya, Johannah and David, Josiah and Allie, Jeremiah and Lizzie—thank you for being understanding and supportive.

Ultimately, if it wasn't for God's call on my life and His anointing upon my life, this book would not have come about. The impartations would not have taken place and the stories would not have occurred and been transcribed. Thank you,

Lord, for letting me be the donkey Jesus sometimes rode on into church services all over the world. Thank you Father, Son, and Holy Spirit. To you, the great triune God, be all the glory and praise.

# CONTENTS

# FOREWORD

*Andrew S. Park*
*Professor of Theology and Ethics*
*United Theological Seminary*

In 1994, the Airport Vineyard Christian Fellowship in Toronto, Canada invited Randy for four nights of meetings. An unparalleled outpouring of the Holy Spirit stretched those four nights into twenty-plus years and continues today. Through the "Toronto Blessing" Randy Clark was sovereignly lifted up and used by God to touch an estimated 1.8 million pastors, leaders, and individuals from approximately 200 countries. Such tidal waves of spiritual anointing represent one of the largest and longest outpourings of the Holy Spirit in history.

By imparting the outpouring of the Holy Spirit to spiritual giants such as Heidi and Rolland Baker and Bill Johnson, to name a few, Randy has greatly contributed to reshaping the contour of world religion by expanding the population of Christians in the world under the guidance of the Holy Spirit. As Randy shares the impartation of the Holy Spirit with millions of people, they in turn pass the impartation on to others, exponentially multiplying Spirit-filled leaders and laypeople around the world, particularly in Latin America. The ripple effect from Randy's ministry may never be fully known this side of heaven.

The resulting Charismatic movement, along with other pentecostal-Charismatic movements, has altered the class structure of many countries. With its healing emphasis, this Charismatic movement has attracted a number of the poor who could not afford medical treatment. When touched and healed by the power of the Holy Spirit, married men changed their lifestyles, became faithful to God and to their spouses, stopped drinking, quit drugs, began to work hard, and became serious for children's education. Because of their changed hearts and lifestyles, within a generation their children received an education and were able to lift themselves out of poverty and move up to a higher social status. As poor families came out of poverty, social class structures were transformed.

In *Authority to Heal*, Randy provides the biblical foundation for healing that counteracts cessationists and other skeptics who believe that miracles and healings ceased since the time of the first apostles. His definitive biblical scholarship and his own personal experiences clearly demonstrate the continuous work of God's healings and miracles in today's world. In the pages of this book, Randy shares the inspirational and moving testimony of his own healing and the resulting transformation that led him into the ministry of healing and has kept him there since. As a part of this transformation, the Lord told him through a strong impression that, "The issue of your lifetime will be the Holy Spirit." This word from the Lord was confirmed by John Wimber's prophecy: "One day [you would] go to the nations to activate the gifts of the Spirit and the baptism of the Spirit by the laying on of hands."

Randy's work is full of the Holy Spirit and of sound theology based upon the Bible. No book has been written by a healing practitioner with academic rigor and scientific verification of healing such as this one. *Authority to Heal* marks an epoch in the history of Christianity. Randy's life work convinces me that my theological teaching based on the intellect is insufficient and inadequate for equipping ministerial students. We all need the spiritual, intellectual, and physical scope of theological education according to Jesus' holistic healing if we are to minister effectively in the world today. What Dr. Clark has written in *Authority to Heal* is truly extraordinary. I have not read such a cogent work as this that verifies healings of the sick with a credible group of medical and social scientists.

I served on Randy Clark's dissertation committee as the faculty consultant at United Theological Seminary, but it is I who learned from him. His teachings and writings woke me from my "dogmatic slumbers" (Kant). I have come to understand the urgent and indispensable need for receiving instruction from the Holy Spirit and learning to work with the Spirit in the midst of practical ministry to others. *Authority to Heal* will significantly help my classroom teaching in this regard.

Appointed by God, Randy Clark is a uniquely genuine and extraordinary charismatic leader of our age. It is rare to see in a person the combination of integrity, strong theological scholarship, and a strong anointing of the Holy Spirit. God has endowed Randy with these gifts. At heart, he is a wounded pastoral healer who loves Jesus and loves people. I have found him to be an authentic, humble, candid, and rumor-free Christian leader. At the same time, he is innately theological, scholarly, well-informed, and brilliant. Randy has a warm and passionate heart for Christ and for people and keeps a cool head for authentic and sound theological viewpoints. This work speaks volumes about the actuality of such a man of God.

# INTRODUCTION

*Jesus went throughout Galilee, teaching in their synagogues, proclaiming the good news of the kingdom, and healing every disease and sickness among the people* (Matthew 4:23).

*A large crowd followed him, and he healed all who were ill* (Matthew 12:15).

Jesus' earthly ministry was characterized by healings, miracles, signs, and wonders. As we read through the gospels, we find Jesus either teaching or healing, or more often doing both. Sometimes we see him attempting to draw away from the crowds to spend time alone with his Father in heaven, but the crowds always seem to find him, and when they do they press in for healing. The lame, the sick, the deaf, the blind, and even those whose loved ones have died come to Jesus. They come on stretchers, are lowered down through holes in the roof, reach out to touch the hem of his garment, lie beside the road calling out to him as he passes by, and are so desperate for healing that they agree to take whatever "crumbs" can be found under his table just to receive his touch.

One of the first things Jesus did when he began his ministry was to gather a small group of disciples around him[1] so that he could train them to do what he was doing. These twelve men lived daily with Jesus, watching in wonder and sometimes confusion as they saw the long promised Messiah fulfilling the words of the prophets of old, bringing the Kingdom of God to bear on the kingdom of this world.

On the night before his crucifixion, as Jesus comforted his disciples, he spoke to them about the promised Holy Spirit (see John 14:15-31), who would come to them and "teach them all things" so that they (the disciples) might continue to do the work that He (Jesus) was doing. Later, when He appeared to the eleven after His resurrection, "He said to them, 'Go into all the world and preach the good news to all creation. …And these signs will accompany those who believe: In my name they will drive out demons; they will speak in new tongues…they will place their hands on sick people, and they will get well'" (Mark 16:15,17-18).

> Just as the early disciples received the empowering of the Holy Spirit and ministered powerfully in the name of Jesus, you can too.

The early Church, as we see it in the remainder of the New Testament beginning with the book of Acts, was indeed empowered by the Holy Spirit (see Acts 2:1–12). These Spirit-filled believers, though few in number and with no resources to speak of, begin to preach the good news of the gospel to a broken and pagan culture, and in a few hundred years the church Jesus established had grown exponentially and reached every part of the known world.

But somewhere along the way the Christian life was stripped of the knowledge of the power and authority of God to heal and of His desire to heal. We lost our spiritual inheritance, our birthright from the finished work of the cross. The good news of the gospel was separated from the power and authority to heal, and we have been struggling ever since to restore healing to its rightful place in the life of every Christian.

Many believers today understand and practice the ministry of healing in the Church, but many more do not, and significant resistance still exists. Long-held beliefs and ideologies stemming from doctrines handed down through the history of the Church have attempted to squelch the truth that the supernatural power of God to heal is available to all believers.

Just as the early disciples received the empowering of the Holy Spirit and ministered powerfully in the name of Jesus, you can too. God is inviting you into the supernatural lifestyle that He intends for all believers. When you accept His invitation, it will transform the way you understand what the Christian faith looks like and how we are to function as Christians in the world today.

Most of you have an understanding of Christian discipline. You know that there are interior disciplines such as solitude, silence, and fasting that God calls us to balance with the disciplines of engagement in the culture and world around us such as worship, fellowship, and service, but have you ever considered that healing can and should be added to the list of Christian disciplines?

I have personally been privileged to minister healing to many over the years, and I know firsthand that healing is a Christian discipline that profoundly impacts both believers and unbelievers alike. Lives are changed forever when God brings His healing touch to bear. There is such joy in seeing someone relieved of years of pain or healed of a debilitating disease, when the deaf hear, the blind see, and the lame walk. These things are happening today, all over the world, as Christian believers reach out with faith in the knowledge that God heals. You too can minister healing. God wants to use you to advance His Kingdom, and He makes His Holy Spirit available to equip you for this task.

After being miraculously healed as a teenager, I made it the mission of my life to impart to others the gifts of the Spirit, to bring healing to people as well as forgiveness of sins. I took Jesus' words literally—to freely give what I have freely received (see Matt. 10:8).

I founded the ministry of Global Awakening, which teaches believers how to pray for the sick, and in the process we have seen thousands miraculously healed. Over the years, I have utilized methods for collecting data about these healings in order to follow up with those who were healed and even to verify their healings. Using academic methods, I recently focused my research specifically on those people with surgically implanted materials who were experiencing pain or range of mobility restrictions as a result of the implanted material.

A professor at Duke University Medical School encouraged me to attempt to verify healing for a specific condition that would be practical to study in the field where there is little access to medical devices. He suggested testing for hearing loss or for vision loss. Dr. Candy Brown and her team had already done this and reported their findings in both the "Study of the Therapeutic Effects of Proximal Intercessory Prayer (STEPP)" article, which appeared in a peer-reviewed medical journal, and in her book, *Testing Prayer: Science and Healing*,[2] so utilizing Global Awakening meetings in the United States and internationally, I decided to move beyond a replicative study into a fresh area of investigation.

The subject for my research needed to be such that I could check for improvement without expensive medical equipment or a hospital context. Chronic pain or loss of range of motion seemed suitable, so I chose these as target areas. Tests involving self-awareness for pain levels and mobility/range-of-motion tests are used by physical therapists as a basis for determining whether further treatment is merited in order to determine if insurance companies will continue to pay for the treatment. I decided I would use the same two tests. The background leading up to my research was extensive, spanning many years.

I became interested in studying surgically implanted materials after attendees at my meetings reported healings from chronic pain and/or restoration of range of motion following surgeries, beginning with cases on September 19, 2009. Prior to that, in August 2009, Pastor Bill Johnson of Bethel Church in Redding, California shared that scores of people for whom he had prayed were claiming they had been "healed" of problems arising from surgeries involving implanted materials. The pain they had had ever since the surgery was now gone and the loss of movement restored. For some, the surgically implanted metal had made such movement previously impossible. Bill did not know whether the metal had disappeared or whether it had somehow changed into a form that now allowed movement. He also shared that some of the people reported that the metal had actually disappeared.

This information from Bill Johnson created a new perspective on what was possible—suddenly the impossible seemed possible. I believe this change in perspective is due to the "renewing of the mind" or having one's "mind transformed" in light of the power of another Kingdom impacting one's life— the Kingdom of Heaven.[3] This concept is illustrated in Romans 12:2 as Paul writes, "Do not conform any longer to the pattern of this world, but be transformed by the renewing of your mind. Then you will be able to test and approve what God's will is—his good, pleasing and perfect will." This type of paradigm shift eliminates the ceiling that limits what we consider to be possible, because what we consider to be possible is typically as much as we will believe God can do.

As I studied the Scriptures from this new perspective[4]—that the seemingly impossible is possible with God—my mind was once again renewed. My understanding of what was possible shifted, and the result was that miracles increased.[5] I realized that not only could God alleviate pain and restore range of motion, but He could make metal disappear. Bill Johnson was seeing this happen. When the unlimited Kingdom of God—a Kingdom of supernatural power—collided with these ailments, pain was supernaturally alleviated. Where doctors could not relieve post-op pain or restore range of motion, God could and did.

In addition to this research, I have spent the last twenty-eight years addressing inadequate biblical discipleship in the Church, which stems from a biblical hermeneutic developed within the theological construct of cessationism, liberalism, or dispensationalism that is unfaithful to the commands of Jesus and the concept of *sola scriptura*. This inadequate discipleship has allowed the traditions of man to negate the commandments of God. Christians are to be equipped for ministry, and this ministry is to include in particular physical healing, inner healing, and deliverance. This mandate for all Christians to walk in supernatural exploits is not peripheral to the gospel; it is integral. Unfortunately, the Church has often settled for less than Jesus' Great Commission made available.

> This mandate for all Christians to walk in supernatural exploits is not peripheral to the gospel; it is integral.

We are familiar with Jesus' mandate to "Go therefore and make disciples of all the nations, baptizing them in the name of the Father and of the Son and of the Holy Spirit" but we tend to ignore His follow-up instructions: "teaching them to observe *all* things that I have commanded you" (Matt. 28:19-20 NKJV). Teaching *what?* All that Jesus commanded. This includes the supernatural ministries of healing of sickness and deliverance from demons. Teaching *who?* Not just first-century apostles or uniquely appointed disciples. This is a multi-generational commission that will continue until the second coming. It is available to *whosoever believes* in Jesus (see John 14:12-13).

I see healing as part of the way in which I carry out the Great Commission. At Global Awakening we focus on training for ministry, developing spiritual gifting, and teaching power evangelism. With our global reach we have ministered in many countries in Europe, Asia, Africa, South America, Central America, and North America. Our methods include crusades of anywhere from 2,000 to 100,000 people; four yearly "schools" of healing and impartation; our Global School of Supernatural Ministry (Global School); a one- or two-year program with a third year internship option; an online and satellite version of Global School; and the Wagner Leadership Institute.

In addition, Global Awakening conducts two major conferences per year (Voice of the Prophets in the Spring, and Voice of the Apostles in the Fall) where ministry for healing and impartation occur. The spring conference has an attendance of about 1,500, and the late summer or fall conference has about 5,000 in attendance. Multiple hundreds of people are healed at these two conferences each year. Many also receive an anointing or gifting for healing.

Our online programs teach biblical and theological foundations as well as church history and practical ministry. The biblical track emphasizes the Bible and its major themes, noting the priority of the power of God in the Scriptures. It is designed to provide a strong underpinning for the importance of discipleship training in healing and deliverance, which I believe is the emphasis of Scripture. God's plan was to establish a charismatic people who could hear Him and cooperate with Him.[6]

During my time as a student in the doctoral program at United Theological Seminary (UTS) in Dayton, Ohio, the school saw that a significant level of interest exists among Charismatic leaders for training in the ministry of healing. As a result, Global Awakening is now working with UTS to develop courses for their new Master of Divinity focus—"World Charismatic Studies." Regent University has also asked us to work with them to develop courses for the practical ministry side of their Master of Divinity degree. In the fall of 2016, the Apostolic Network of Global Awakening will work with Family of Faith College and its supportive apostolic network of churches to form the Global Awakening Theological Seminary of Family of Faith College. It will have U.S. Dept. of Ed. recognition with accreditation by the Association of Biblical Higher Education.

As I go about equipping the saints for the work of ministry, it is my great desire to see the Church fully operate as the empowered body of Jesus Christ in the earth today. To that end, together in this book we will examine our authority to heal from a biblical perspective, how the Church lost this knowledge, and how we can continue to regain it today to help the body of Christ operate as God intends. So much has been made available to the Church. We as believers should not be willing to settle for less. The authority of Jesus to heal can be fully restored in this generation and for generations to come. Let us press in vigorously for the "more" that God has for us.

# PART ONE

# MARKED BY HIS POWER

# Chapter 1

# A CHILDHOOD SHAPED BY HEALING

I have been continuously involved in the ministry of praying for the sick since 1984, affording me a relatively extensive breadth of experience. From this unique position I have seen healing in the real-world setting of active ministry. I have spent over twenty-eight years gaining a better understanding of the variables that can affect the probability of healing, going back constantly to the pages of Scripture to find the truth of God's word, and to the halls of history to understand healing in the context of the evolving Church. In the process I have seen what it looks like to restore the lost birthright that is our authority to heal the sick in Jesus' name.

I have found over the years that a lot of people are drawn to the ministry of healing because they have been healed and seen others healed. That is in large part true for me. I was born in 1952, the first of three children. My mother was eighteen and my father was twenty at the time of my birth. I lived in a nuclear family, and my childhood was rooted and blessed with love, stability, and Christian values. I was raised in the church, attending services twice on Sunday and once midweek, every week. Yet even against the backdrop of family and faith, there were things to overcome.

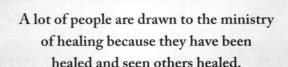

A lot of people are drawn to the ministry
of healing because they have been
healed and seen others healed.

I grew up in one of the fifty poorest counties in the United
States—Hamilton County, Illinois. My dad had an eighth
grade education and my maternal grandmother was illiterate.
I can remember feeling guilty because my dad couldn't afford
to buy shoes often enough to keep up with my rapidly growing
feet. Poverty can impact you in many ways, and the lack in our
lives taught me how to be an overcomer, which has served me
well throughout my life.

When I was about two years old my maternal grandfather
experienced a radical conversion that delivered him from alco-
hol addiction and a lifestyle of infidelity. He and my father
were converted side by side on the same night. My grandfather became a devoted Christian who loved God and a man
of prayer and compassion. I would sit next to him often in the
little country Baptist church we attended. When he was six-
ty-two he died of colon and bone cancer. I was sixteen at the
time, and seeing my grandfather die even though many had
prayed for his healing confused me. Just four years earlier I had
seen my Sunday school teacher healed of a large tumor after
much prayer. I was amazed by her story and believed she had
been healed because of her saintliness. I thought at the time
she was one of the most spiritual individuals I had ever known,
in addition to my maternal grandmother. You can see how my

adolescent theology developed—I basically believed that healing was associated with saintliness!

To add to my confusion was the story of my maternal grandmother's unique healing. My maternal grandmother had a profound impact upon my spiritual development. She was illiterate, only able to write her name and read a stop sign, but she could hear God speaking to her internally, and a few times audibly. When I was about five years old she told me her story of healing. She had a large goiter, but the doctors did not know how to treat that condition back then, and so she suffered. One day, the audible voice of God told her to "go into the other bedroom and pray," and He would heal her. When she simply obeyed the voice, she felt what she described as a "hot hand" go down into her throat causing the goiter to instantly vanish. Her healing story made a strong impression on my young mind.

I first came under the Holy Spirit's conviction at the age of seven. The weight of God's conviction on my young heart would make me cry, and embarrassed by my tears I would roll over in the pew so no one could see me crying. As time went by, I hardened my heart until I couldn't feel His conviction any longer. But God wouldn't let me go. My hard heart began to trouble me, so much so that I asked God to bring His conviction upon me once again. God always hears us, and He heard me and answered.

At the age of sixteen I had a dramatic conversion experience that was so powerful I knew beyond a shadow of a doubt that I had been saved by the work of Jesus on the cross. This was a "born again" experience. In John 3, Jesus tells Nicodemus that no one can enter the Kingdom of God unless he is born of water and the Spirit, and that each one of us must be born again so that we can become children of God (see John 3:3–7; John 1:12-13).

By the time I was eighteen I had experienced three close brushes with death. At the age of seven I was kicked in the head by a horse. Had his hoof landed an inch or two in a different direction I would have likely died. In the sixth grade I cut an artery clean in two while shucking corn by hand in the field. Then, at eighteen I came very close to dying in a car accident that took the life of my dear friend.

I was driving the car when it happened. Three friends were with me, two of them my best friends. A car passed us and lost control, sliding into the side of my car and knocking us off the road. I don't remember much after that, but I was told my car went about fifty feet before it hit a concrete embankment, flipped end over end, hit a pole, and landed in a ditch. My good friend was killed, his sister was severely injured, and my other friend had only minor injuries. I was badly hurt.

I had crushed facial bones, broken ribs, and a paralyzed digestive tract. I also had nerve damage from compressed discs in my spine. It took sixty stitches to sew up the lacerations on my face. The doctors said I would be in the hospital anywhere from seven to eleven weeks. People from my church came to pray for me, and right before I was to be transferred to another hospital to better deal with my injuries, tests revealed that my digestive tract was no longer paralyzed. I believe this was a result of their prayers.

That same day, a doctor came to set my broken jaw but couldn't because it had healed! A short time later all of the pain left my spine. The pain had been so bad I needed fifty milligrams of Demerol, a morphine derivative, every three hours.

I was not allowed to move because there was a great risk of paralysis. I was not even allowed to have a pillow. All I could do was lay there.

Somewhere between the twelfth and fifteenth day of my hospitalization I had a strong impression from God that I was healed and that I was supposed to get out of bed. It was such a strong impression that I trusted God and got out of the bed and stood up despite all the doctor's orders. Of course, the nurses were very upset with me, but I refused to get back into bed. I knew I was healed, and I was! I left the hospital shortly afterward. The realization that God had healed me was immediately followed by a profound realization that God had a purpose for my life. At nineteen I became a licensed minister of the gospel, and at twenty-one I was ordained.

My most recent experience with healing came in 2008, thirty-eight years later. I was at home, in the middle of a meeting with my pastoral advisors, and when I tried to stand up excruciating pain shot through my back. I hadn't experienced anything like it since the car accident. The doctor diagnosed neurological damage to my spine caused by years of international flying. I had classic "traveler's back" in which the lower lumbar (where the spine curves) had degenerated to the point that the base of my spine was now flat instead of curved. Because of this, the discs in my back slipped easily. My doctor recommended I stop flying.

I couldn't put any pressure on my leg without severe pain. The doctor prescribed painkillers and anti-inflammatories. Even the slightest movement of my hip brought excruciating pain. I had three herniated discs and two pinched nerves and arthritis of the spine. Physical therapy and pain medication helped minimally, but for the most part I was reduced to lying on a mat or in bed. I received two epidurals to no avail, and back surgery began to look like my only alternative.

I am grateful for the good medical care I received, but relief from the pain and restoration of movement in my back came as a result of prayer. I received prayer from friends who were known for strong healing gifts, but I wasn't healed. The prayers that healed me came through two people who are not noted for healing. One was my oldest son Josh, who was out of the country at the time. He prayed for me and I received partial healing. The rest of my healing came through a businessman in Louisiana, Ray Smith. God gave Ray an open vision of my back in which he saw the spine and the nerves going out of the spine. Then he saw Jesus, who showed him specifically how to pray for my condition. Ray prayed exactly as Jesus instructed, then he sent me an e-mail detailing the open vision and his prayers, but I was asleep and didn't see his e-mail until the next day, after I was healed. I woke up that morning and discovered I could walk without crutches, go up and down the stairs, and all the pain was gone. God miraculously healed me. I still travel over 200 days out of the year, often on flights of fifteen hours or more.

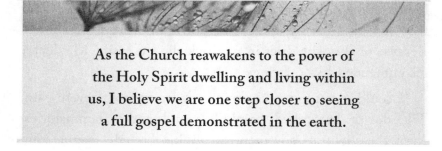

As the Church reawakens to the power of
the Holy Spirit dwelling and living within
us, I believe we are one step closer to seeing
a full gospel demonstrated in the earth.

My own personal healing experiences took me out of academic thinking and put me firmly in a place of understanding that God has always intended the ministry of healing to be a normative part of the life of the Church. When I needed healing for my back, the question of whether or not healing and the gifts of the Spirit are available today was more than an academic question to me; I *needed* healing or I would have to have surgery. My healing experiences helped me to understand that it is God's desire that every believer pray for the sick, not just those in leadership. Although I requested prayer from those who operated in notable healing gifts, my pain was healed through those who were not recognized as apostolic "healers" and who were not recognized for flowing in a gift of healing. My physical injuries and subsequent healing also helped me when I began to conduct more formal research in the issue of healing prayer. Because I was well versed personally in what it means to test for pain, I was able to construct reliable methods of gaging the impact of healing prayer on pain levels and range of motion.

Today, I believe healing is central to the gospel much more strongly than I did in the 1970s when I began in ministry. In fact, this pursuit after the importance of God's healing power is central to my ministry today. As the Church reawakens to the power of the Holy Spirit dwelling and living within us, I believe we are one step closer to seeing a *full* gospel demonstrated in the earth.

# CHAPTER 2

# FROM HEALED TO HEALING MINISTRY

Early on in my ministry, I received a directive from the Lord that the Holy Spirit would be *the issue* of my life. This has been very evident, as my vision is to help activate Christians to walk in the supernatural power of God as their normative expression of faith, knowing that this can only be accomplished through the Holy Spirit.

I use the word *normative* here because lifestyles characterized by manifestations of God's power have become the exception for the Church, not the standard. They are mistakenly labeled as "abnormal" when, in fact, the standard for the early Church was supernatural. Those who experience the miraculous in the Church today are often seen as outlandish, strange, or weird when measured next to the contemporary standard of what Christianity *should* look like in a twenty-first century context.

Even though we have this unfortunate history in the Church, the tides are turning. More and more people are pressing in to experience the fullness of the Kingdom, which cannot happen outside of the supernatural power of God. Across the earth, hungry hearts are crying out to God, saying, *"There must be more."*

The good news is that there is more, and His name is Holy Spirit. I met Him in a transformative way as a young man, and now He has graced me—a truly broken vessel—to be a catalyst in imparting gifts of the Spirit into Christ-followers worldwide. It is not too late to restore our lost inheritance of God's healing power in the Church. Restoration begins by understanding what we lost and how we lost it.

As a student in Baptist seminary, I continued to be faithful to God's word to me that the Holy Spirit would be the issue of my life. This was not always easy. While taking a course on the book of Acts, I needed to write a term paper. There were about fifty possible subjects to write on, but healing was not among them. I had to ask for special permission to write on healing, and thankfully it was granted. The professor had one condition—my paper had to be academic not anecdotal. He didn't want stories; he wanted research. The problem was, there was little in the seminary library on healing. I found a few books at the Baptist library and another good book at the Presbyterian library and wrote my paper.[1]

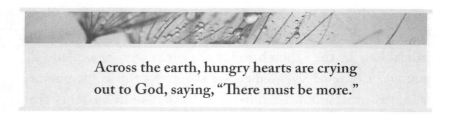

Across the earth, hungry hearts are crying out to God, saying, "There must be more."

In reviewing my paper, the professor said to me, "You have written this paper as if healing is central to the gospel.[2] It is not. Healing is only peripheral to the gospel. If you continue down this path of thinking and speaking you will have problems in the Baptist churches." In spite of my professor's warning, I would not back down from what I thought to be true. Today I believe more strongly than I did back in 1976 that healing is central, not peripheral to the gospel. This pursuit has followed me into adulthood and shaped my ministry.

When a person is faced with injury or illness, all else can fade to the periphery of their life. Our health, good or bad, impacts every aspect of living. Have you wondered why there is such a proliferation of alternative healing methods today? People are desperate for healing, and when they can't find it in traditional allopathic medicine or the Church they turn to other methods that can be ungodly. The phenomenal growth of New Age practices such as Reiki, Therapeutic Touch (TT), and Healing Touch in America is a sign of the interest in non-traditional means of healing. The New Age movement's interest in healing is contributing to its fast growth.[3] How is the Church to respond to this?

We begin by restoring the ministry of healing to the Church today in the power of the Holy Spirit, so that divine healing can be available to work in conjunction with traditional medicine. Divine healing as a part of health care has been, is, and will continue to be an urgent matter to individuals and to nations.[4] Think on this— if the Church awakens to its divine mandate, which includes healing, it could save the government billions of tax dollars each year for health care.[5]

The Church in America has allowed religious traditions to cause the commands of God to be ignored. In Mark 7:8 Jesus said, "You have let go of the commands of God and are holding on to the traditions of men." As a religious culture, we have settled for too little when it comes to our biblical inheritance in Christ. The miraculous should be a lifestyle for everyone who follows Christ, yet when you consider the present state of

Christianity it is easy to question this statement. Even if we say that the miraculous should be normal in the Church today, the fact that it isn't leads us to ask, "Why not?" and "How can we get back there as the body of Christ?" To discover how to sustain a supernatural lifestyle, where God's healing power flows in a normative manner, we need to go back into the Scriptures where we will find a clear blueprint for God's original will and intent.

> If you have ever wondered why people
> are leaving the Church—particularly
> young people—and searching elsewhere
> for spiritual power, it is because they have
> encountered a false, powerless gospel.

This journey back to the supernatural lifestyle of the believer includes an examination of the history of the Church as it pertains to the lost ministry of healing, because we must pursue both the information and the revelation.

Doctrines have circulated in the Church throughout history, attempting to convince believers that the supernatural power of God is not available to us. This is liberal theology, which is easily recognizable by its deceptive perspective that does not recognize the miracles in Scripture. These anti-healing doctrines are ideologies that have stripped the Christian life of power and potency. They reduce discipleship to a prayer, while attempting to adhere to a moral lifestyle, and the inevitable death that ultimately leads to salvation in heaven. This is a powerless gospel.

If you have ever wondered why people are leaving the Church—particularly young people—and searching elsewhere for spiritual power, it is because they have encountered a false, powerless gospel. They are being denied their spiritual inheritance in Christ, where healing, deliverance, and the demonstration of God's power are inextricably linked to the gospel of the Kingdom of God. A perfect example of this can be found in the testimony of Martha Wertz in Chapter Eleven. Martha thought she had found the "power" to minister healing in occult New Age practices. In Matthew 10:7-8, Jesus made this essential connection when he commissioned the apostles, saying, "As you go, preach, saying, 'The kingdom of heaven is at hand.' Heal the sick, cleanse the lepers, raise the dead, cast out demons. Freely you have received, freely give" (NKJV).

Eternal salvation is our entrance into the Kingdom of God. When we are born again, we are saved from our sins, filled with the Holy Spirit, and adopted into a family that is the Kingdom. While I cannot overemphasize the importance of salvation, I likewise cannot overemphasize the need to disciple Christians to actually live out a Kingdom lifestyle. Once more, this is why a generation remains disconnected from church culture. Techniques don't win them. Gimmicks do not sustain their commitment. Fads do not feed the cry of their hearts. They know that there must be more to following Jesus than a prayer and a "get into heaven" pass.

We are not to devalue the cardinal doctrines of the faith, teaching that healing and miracles are more important that salvation or deserve emphasis above the redemptive work of Jesus. At the same time, the neglect of the miraculous has, in many ways, denied Jesus of the glory that He deserves. This is the end we are working toward. It's not healing for healing's sake. Every miracle reveals the nature of the Miracle Worker and thus fulfills the very mandate of God's heart: "but indeed, as I live, all the earth will be filled with the glory of the Lord" (Num. 14:21 NASB).

## RESTORING THE MANDATE TO HEAL OTHERS

Throughout my research and over the course of my life, I have found that too often God is perceived as unwilling to heal because of a misunderstanding of His divine sovereignty. God's will *is* healing. The deeper issue is more often a widely held theology of unbelief, which causes a lowered expectation to receive healing. Unfortunately, this issue has prevailed throughout much of the history of the Church. Rather than recognizing a widespread assent to unbelief in the miraculous and faithlessness for the supernatural, Christians—even notable church fathers—constructed theologies that accommodated powerlessness.

These church fathers and pioneers are key pillars in church history and worthy of honor. They defended key doctrines against heresy, surrendered their lives for the global expansion of the gospel, and sacrificed immeasurably so that the Church of today could stand firmly on the theological foundation they secured. While we should rightly give recognition to these catalytic efforts, the truth is that many of these same individuals also propagated inaccurate information about the continuation of spiritual gifts and the demonstration of God's power.

In the same manner that theological cornerstones such as the divinity of Christ and the atonement were established, so were subtle strongholds of deception concerning the miraculous. Because of the subtle integration of unbelief and cessationism, the widespread expectation of the Church became one of unbelief instead of expectation when it came to the miraculous. One of the most obvious examples of this is found in the Westminster Confession of Faith. This confession first appeared in 1647 and makes clear in its opening paragraph how this group of reformed thinkers felt about the gifts of the Spirit. It reads:

> Therefore it pleased the Lord, at sundry times, and in divers manners, to reveal himself, and to declare that his will unto his church; and afterwards, for the better preserving and propagating of the truth, and for the more sure establishment and comfort of the church against the corruption of the flesh, and the malice of Satan and of the world, to commit the same wholly unto writing: which maketh the Holy Scripture to be most necessary; those former ways of God's revealing his will unto his people being now ceased.

The modern 1993 version reveals a belief that, having received the canon of Scripture, there is no need for further revelation from the Lord.

> Therefore the Holy Scripture is most necessary, God's former ways of revealing his will to his people having ceased.

And it is re-emphasized in paragraph 10 of the opening chapter as well:

> The supreme judge by whom all controversies of religion are to be settled and all decrees of councils,

opinions of ancient writers, doctrines of men, and claims to private revelations are to be examined, can be only the Holy Spirit speaking in the Scripture. With his decision we are to be satisfied.

## EXPECTATION AND THE MIRACULOUS

My considerable exposure to hundreds of thousands of meeting attendees each year has revealed that, in addition to one's theological beliefs, biblical and historical beliefs as well as personal experience are all variables that positively or negatively affect the probability of receiving healing. These factors will either increase or decrease one's expectation for the supernatural. This is why I view expectation as such an important variable. I am amazed at how expectation can be increased in those present in a meeting by teaching, videos, worship, and the testimonies of others who experienced healing.

I have found that personal theology, expectation, and personal experience of healing all prove to be key factors for healing. When these variables are incorporated they can actually create an atmosphere charged with faith and expectation for the miraculous—on the one hand. On the other hand, when cessationist teaching is accompanied by stories of failed attempts at healing and coupled with a focus on what some perceive God is *not* doing, a distorted theology comes into play causing expectation to diminish.

I believe wholeheartedly that people are in fact being healed across the globe, not only of pain and/or mobility restrictions resulting from pain and movement restriction, but from all types of ailments and maladies—cancer, post-traumatic stress disorder (PTSD), fibromyalgia, blindness, and deafness, just to name a few. I see these healings in my own ministry and in the ministry of many others such as Heidi and Rolland Baker, Bill Johnson, the other members of the Revival Alliance, and in several other ministries today, not to mention significant ministries of healing from the past.

Through my teaching and writing, I want to help stir the body of Christ to a place of expectation for the miraculous once again. This is our lost birthright that we are to reclaim as we rediscover our authority to heal in Jesus' name. When Jesus walked the earth, those who needed a miracle *expected* something from Him. As a result, they approached Him from a posture of expectation. It was expectation that caused a woman with a twelve-yearlong blood hemorrhage to press through a crowd and simply touch the hem of Jesus' garment. She was healed—we know this much. I am amazed at the level of expectation she had. It compelled her to press through a crowd, possibly humiliate herself, and take a tremendous risk (see Luke 8:43–48). Jesus rewarded her risk with healing.

Blind Bartimaeus heard that Jesus was soon to pass by and cried out, "Jesus, Son of David, have mercy on me!" (Mark 10:47 NKJV). When people tried to silence him, he cried out all the louder, compelled by an expectation that the Man passing by, the Son of David, would restore his sight. Scripture makes it clear that, because of the blind man's faith and expectation in Jesus, he was made well (see Mark 10:51-52).

This expectation was not limited to the earthly ministry of Jesus. His miraculous works continued through the early Church, as revealed in the book of Acts. From the Church's very beginning, we read of expectation that was met with the miraculous. Consider this notable miracle that was a powerful catalyst in the expansion of the Church:

*Now Peter and John went up together to the temple at the hour of prayer, the ninth hour. And a certain man lame from his mother's womb was carried, whom they laid daily at the gate of the temple which is called Beautiful, to ask alms from those who entered the temple; who, seeing Peter and John about to go into the temple, asked for alms. And fixing his eyes on him, with John, Peter said, "Look at us." So he gave them his attention, expecting to receive something from them* (Acts 3:1–5 NKJV).

Note the posture of the lame man: "he gave them his attention, expecting to receive." Most likely, he was expecting a financial offering. Peter made it very clear that what he offered was infinitely greater than "silver and gold" and, in turn, used the authority of Jesus' name to see this man miraculously healed. Expectation is everything when it comes to receiving the miraculous.

God intends for the Church to fully operate as the empowered body of Jesus Christ in the earth. In order for this to be accomplished, believers must be activated in the gifts and anointing of the Holy Spirit.

Even the early Church, beyond the book of Acts, expected the manifestation of divine healing for the first 300 years of church history. They expected gifts of the Spirit, prophetic utterance, and speaking in tongues when they were water baptized, believing that this also included a baptism in the Holy Spirit. They expected that Jesus' words still rang true—that healing, deliverance, and supernatural exploits would be performed by their anointed hands. This early faith community recognized that they were not working the miracles; rather, they understood their role as conduits through whom the Spirit of God could freely flow.

Sadly, this flow became restricted over the centuries, not due to God's sovereignty or willingness, but because those who were entrusted with His power had, by choice, shut it down. It is past time to see our lost inheritance fully restored and fully active in the life of every single Christian.

## CALLING FORTH THE ANOINTED BODY OF CHRIST

God intends for the Church to fully operate as the empowered body of Jesus Christ in the earth. In order for this to be accomplished, believers must be activated in the gifts and anointing of the Holy Spirit. Healing and deliverance are part of the primary acts of service that Jesus rendered. Jesus' preaching taught freedom from spiritual death, damnation, disease, demonization, and despair. He offered healing, hope, holiness, freedom from demonic oppression, and heaven.

In order to see the power ministry of Jesus continue on earth, through the Church, there must be a dependency upon the person and work of the Holy Spirit. It is the Holy Spirit that Jesus promised to His people, claiming that the One who was to come (the Holy Spirit) would actually put us at an advantage (see John 16:7)—those who would receive the Holy Spirit would be in a better place than they were when He (Jesus) actually walked among them in physical form. As long as Jesus walked the earth, He could only be in one place at one time. Once He died, rose again, and ascended into heaven, He opened the way for every single person who called upon the saving name of Jesus—from generation to generation—to become indwelt by God and filled with His power.

While on earth, Jesus' physical body brought healing and deliverance to those with whom He came into contact. Through the Holy Spirit in us, we—the present body of Christ—should be doing the same works and witnessing the same results as Jesus. This is why Jesus said, "I assure you, most solemnly I tell you, if anyone steadfastly believes in Me, he will himself be able to do the things that I do; and he will do even greater things than these, because I go to the Father" (John 14:12 AMP).

Problematically, many Christians casually observe promises like this instead of taking them literally. They either assign a false theological context to John 14:12, claiming that Jesus was issuing this promise to the twelve apostles, or they reduce the expression of these works so that they are no longer miraculous in demonstration.[6] The fact remains that Jesus was introducing both His disciples and future generations of Christians to a reality that, because of the indwelling Spirit, they too would be able to demonstrate the miraculous works that Jesus did. The word *works* should be understood in a context of signs, wonders, and healings.

So much has been made available to us as the body of Christ, and yet we have historically settled for so little. It is time to restore Jesus' authority to heal in this current generation—time for the body of Christ to operate fully in our

God-given identity, and we can begin this process of restoration by revisiting the clear biblical and theological basis for divine healing.

# PART TWO

# FOUNDATIONS FOR DIVINE HEALING

# CHAPTER 3

# BIBLICAL FOUNDATIONS FOR HEALING

*And as you go, preach, saying, "The*
*kingdom of heaven is at hand." Heal the*
*sick, cleanse the lepers, raise the dead, cast*
*out demons. Freely you have received,*
*freely give* (Matthew 10:7-8 NKJV).

Healing flows from the very nature of God. In the book of Exodus, God reveals himself as Yahweh-*Ropheh*, "the Lord who heals you."[1] He says, "If you listen carefully to the voice of the Lord your God and do what is right in his eyes, if you pay attention to his commands and keep all his decrees, I will not bring on you any of the diseases I brought on the Egyptians, for I am the Lord, who heals you" (Exod. 15:26).

Healing, though present in the Old Testament, was more of a stream when compared to the flood of healing we see in the New Testament.[2] Yahweh-*Ropheh* healed through Moses, the lawgiver, and through many of His prophets, especially Elijah and Elisha. These men were "types" of Jesus, the Messiah who was to come, who brought the in-break of the Kingdom of God with its healing power.[3] This healing power and its accompanying miracles were prophetic indicators to help the people of Israel recognize their Messiah.

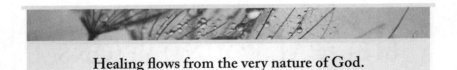

Healing flows from the very nature of God.

*John's disciples told him about all these things. Calling two of them, he sent them to the Lord to ask, "Are you the one who was to come, or should we expect someone else?" When the men came to Jesus, they said, "John the Baptist sent us to you to ask, 'Are you the one who was to come, or should we expect someone else?'" At that very time Jesus cured many who had diseases, sicknesses and evil spirits, and gave sight to many who were blind. So he replied to the messengers, "Go back and report to John what you have seen and heard: The blind receive sight, the lame walk, those who have leprosy are cured, the deaf hear, the dead are raised, and the good news is preached to the poor. Blessed is the man who does not fall away on account of me" (Luke 7:18–23).*

Jesus confirms His identity when He quotes Messianic prophecies in relationship to Himself in Isaiah chapters 35 and 61, and in His ministry to the sick and demonized in Nazareth as found in Luke chapter 4. "Strengthen the feeble hands, steady the knees that give way; say to those with fearful hearts, 'Be strong, do not fear; your God will come, he will come with vengeance; with divine retribution he will come to save you.'

Then will the eyes of the blind be opened and the ears of the deaf unstopped. Then will the lame leap like a deer, and the mute tongue shout for joy. Water will gush forth in the wilderness and streams in the desert" (Isa. 35:3–6).

Later on, Isaiah offers the following words that were announced by Jesus at the inauguration of His ministry: "The Spirit of the Sovereign Lord is on me, because the Lord has anointed me to preach good news to the poor. He has sent me to bind up the brokenhearted, to proclaim freedom for the captives and release from darkness for the prisoners, to proclaim the year of the Lord's favor" (Isa. 61:1-2). Consider the similarity between the Old Testament prophetic oracle in Isaiah and the announcement of Jesus: "The Spirit of the Lord is on me, because he has anointed me to preach good news to the poor. He has sent me to proclaim freedom for the prisoners and recovery of sight for the blind, to release the oppressed, to proclaim the year of the Lord's favor" (Luke 4:18-19).

When imprisonment tested the faith of John the Baptist and John sent his disciples to question Jesus about whether He was the Messiah, Jesus answered him by pointing to the fulfillment of many of the prophetic statements listed in the prophecies of Isaiah 35 and 61.

*When the men came to Jesus, they said, "John the Baptist sent us to you to ask, 'Are you the one who was to come, or should we expect someone else?'" At that very time Jesus cured many who had diseases, sicknesses and evil spirits, and gave sight to many who were blind. So he replied to the messengers, "Go back and report to John what you have seen and heard: The blind receive sight, the lame walk, those who have leprosy are cured, the deaf hear, the dead are raised, and the good news is preached to the poor. Blessed is the man who does not fall away on account of me"* (Luke 7:20–23).

## JESUS COMMISSIONED ALL BELIEVERS TO HEAL THE SICK

Jesus clearly states that believers are to be commissioned to heal the sick.[4] He taught and commanded His disciples to heal the sick, and He directed them to pass this spiritual discipline on to all believers. This is visualized in the progressive commissioning of the twelve, then the seventy, and ultimately the Great Commission. Matthew 10:8 states, "Heal the sick, raise the dead, cleanse those who have leprosy, drive out demons. Freely you have received, freely give." This mandate was not exclusive to the apostles or the first-century Church—it was extended to *whosoever believes* in Jesus (see John 14:12-13).

In Matthew 28:18–20 we find what is often identified as the *Great Commission*. I agree with Dr. Jon Ruthven who sees this *great* commission in light of the other gospel commissionings of the twelve and the seventy. The previous commissionings are to be understood as paradigms of how to interpret and appropriately apply the Great Commission: "Then Jesus came to them and said, 'All authority in heaven and on earth has been given to me. Therefore go and make disciples of all nations, baptizing them in the name of the Father and of the Son and of the Holy Spirit, *and teaching them to obey everything I have commanded you.* And surely I am with you always, to the very end of the age'" (Matt. 28:18–20).

Bishop John Howe in his book *Anointed by the Spirit* notes the word *go* in the Great Commission: "*Go* therefore and make disciples of all nations" and says, "If the authority was given to *him*, [Jesus] why did he command his *disciples* to "go"? Because they were to go *with his authority* and with the enabling of the same Holy Spirit who enabled him.... In effect, he [Jesus] said that the key to his [Jesus'] ministry would also be the key to theirs."[5]

> The primary basis for divine healing
> is threefold and consists of the
> covenant, the cross (or atonement),
> and the Kingdom of God.

What is the scope of divine healing? What possibilities for healing were the disciples to believe for or expect to happen? Jesus said, "Everything is possible for him who believes" (Mark 9:23). This is consistent with the Old Testament, where we see the work of redemption covering sins, for salvation through forgiveness, and physical healing of the body. In the Psalms, we see a promise that reveals the scope of healing available to the believer. "Praise the Lord, O my soul, and forget not all his benefits—who forgives all your sins and heals all your diseases" (Ps. 103:2-3). Dr. Michael L. Brown writes that the nature of salvation in the Old Testament was holistic, affecting both the spirit and the body of those experiencing redemption.[6]

If the scope of divine healing includes all believers, what then is the basis for healing? The primary basis for divine healing is threefold and consists of the covenant, the cross (or atonement), and the Kingdom of God. Scripture tells us that signs and wonders (which accompany healing) are a part of both the Old and New Covenants.

> Then the Lord said: "I am making a covenant with you. Before all your people I will do wonders never before done in any nation in all the world. The people you live among will see how awesome is the work that I, the Lord, will do for you" (Exodus 34:10).

While "wonders" include healings, wonders can also be greater than healings and more expansive in definition and include other types of miracles, such as miracles that transform nature and matter (melting metal implanted in someone's body). Let me share an account of a healing along these lines that occurred in December 2015 at one of our meetings in Brazil. We prayed for healing for people who had metal implanted in their bodies and then called for those who had experienced a touch from God. A man came forward who had a metal bar implanted in his left shoulder, which was attached to a metal string that connected his arm and shoulder to the rest of his body. As a result of this surgery, he had a large scar and metal protruded, forming a bump the size of an olive. After the time of prayer, the bump had disappeared and he could no longer feel the metal. His pain was gone, and movement had been restored so that he could now rotate his arm.[7]

## COVENANT AND ATONEMENT

In Hebrews 2:3-4 we find divine healing based in covenant. "How shall we escape if we ignore such a great salvation? This salvation, which was first announced by the Lord, was confirmed to us by those who heard him. God also testified to it by signs, wonders and various miracles, and gifts of the Holy Spirit distributed according to his will." Hebrews 8:6 continues, "But the ministry Jesus has received is as superior to theirs as the covenant of which he is mediator is superior to the old one, and it is founded on better promises." Some of the Scriptures indicate that healing is included in the covenant between God and his people, while other Scriptures indicate that healing is also in the cross or the atonement.

Matthew 8:17 and First Peter 2:24 clearly relate healing to the blood atonement of Jesus as prophesied in Isaiah 53. Matthew 8:17 is clearly based on Isaiah 53.

> *Surely he took up our infirmities* [sicknesses, Hebrew: kholi—sickness, disease, infirmity (noun form of khalah, to be sick or ill)] *and carried our sorrows* [mental, emotional pain, Hebrew: makh'ov—mental pain, emotional anguish], *yet we considered him stricken by God, smitten by him, and afflicted. But he was pierced for our transgressions, he was crushed for our iniquities; the punishment that brought us peace was upon him, and by his wounds we are healed* (Isaiah 53:4-5).

> *When evening came, many who were demon-possessed were brought to him, and he drove out the spirits with a word and healed all the sick. This was to fulfill what was spoken through the prophet Isaiah: "He took up our infirmities and carried our diseases"* (Matthew 8:16-17).

This Scripture passage from the Septuagint, the Greek translation of the Old Testament, uses the word *sorrows* for diseases. Other translations of the Old Testament used *pains* instead of sorrows.

First Peter 2:24 quotes Isaiah 53 as well, but in doing so changes the verb to the past tense. "He himself bore our sins in his body on the tree, so that we might die to sins and live for righteousness; by his wounds you have been healed."

Whether Peter had a theology of healing as a finished work accomplished already on the cross is a subject that could be debated. Perhaps he merely means that the people to whom he was writing had already experienced healings in their lives, and the statement is a statement of fact and not intended to be taken as a theological statement on the finished work.

## THE KINGDOM OF GOD

The third basis for healing is the *Kingdom of God*. Luke sees physical healing and deliverance as illustrations that the Kingdom of God was beginning to manifest in the earth. "Heal the sick who are there and tell them, 'The kingdom of God is near you'" (Luke 10:9). "But if I drive out demons by the finger of God, then the kingdom of God has come to you" (Luke 11:20).

Luke saw this Kingdom as already present—people were already pressing into it. "The Law and the Prophets were proclaimed until John. Since that time, the good news of the kingdom of God is being preached, and everyone is forcing his way into it" (Luke 16:16).

Luke reveals Jesus' understanding that the Kingdom of God was in us. "Once, having been asked by the Pharisees when the kingdom of God would come, Jesus replied, 'The kingdom of God does not come with your careful observation, nor will people say, "Here it is," or "There it is," because the kingdom of God is within you'" (Luke 17:20-21).

The apostle Paul also understood the dynamic power of the Kingdom of God. He refers to this power in First Corinthians 2:4-5, "My message and my preaching were not with wise and persuasive words, but with a demonstration of the Spirit's power, so that your faith might not rest on men's wisdom, but on God's power."

Again in First Corinthians 4:20 Paul emphasizes the connection between the Kingdom of God and power: "For the kingdom of God is not a matter of talk but of power." Though not using the phrase *Kingdom of God*, he refers to the gospel of Christ—which was a synonym for the gospel of the Kingdom—in his letter to the Romans.

> *Therefore I glory in Christ Jesus in my service to God. I will not venture to speak of anything except what Christ has accomplished through me in leading the Gentiles to obey God by what I have said and done— by the power of signs and miracles, through the power of the Spirit. So from Jerusalem all the way around to Illyricum, I have fully proclaimed the gospel of Christ* (Romans 15:17–19).

In all, there are 278 references to power in the Bible, with most referring to the power of God. Sixty-four of these references are in the New Testament, with Paul using the term fifty-four times, demonstrating a strong understanding of the power or *dunamis* of God and its relationship to the working or energy, *energia,* of God. This is seen most clearly in the NIV translation of Colossians 1:29, "To this end I labor, struggling with all his *energy*, which so powerfully works in me."

The Trinity itself demonstrates God's intention that His Church operate in power and authority through the exercise of the supernatural gifts of the Spirit, including healing and the working of miracles. God the Father sent Jesus the Son, who modeled for us how to live a supernatural lifestyle, and when in the fullness of God's time Jesus rose from the dead to take His place at the right hand of the Father, He sent the Holy Spirit to empower His Church and continue the work Jesus began. We need look no further than the Bible to see the biblical basis for the continuation of spiritual gifts, but in order to do so, many must make their way past the confusion created by the enemy of our souls who labors tirelessly to keep the Church as powerless as possible.

CHAPTER 4

# BIBLICAL BASIS FOR THE CONTINUATION OF SPIRITUAL GIFTS

The enemy has vehemently opposed the contemporary relevance of the gifts of the Spirit by throwing many confusing philosophies against this truth that are not of God. In order for the Church as a whole to see the ministry of healing restored, there must be a biblical return to the availability and authority of the supernatural.

This biblical return to the supernatural as normative in the life of believers can begin with an examination of the scriptural basis for the continuation of the gifts, including healing and working of miracles throughout the history of the Church. The Bible teaches that the gifts are to continue until Jesus returns. Furthermore, it was not expected that they would end with the death of the apostles or with the completion of the Bible.

We know that the Great Commission indicates that people who become Christians are supposed to be taught how to do what Jesus taught His disciples to do. Additionally, Jesus' parables about the Kingdom of Heaven imply that the gifts are to continue. When you examine the parables in Matthew 13—the parable of the sower and the seed, the parable of the mustard seed, and the yeast and the dough—you see that each one teaches about the ongoing increase of the Kingdom of God. Nowhere does Jesus seem to indicate that the Kingdom will inaugurate with power and great growth but will sputter and lose its energies of grace—the gifts of the Spirit—as history unfolds.

> The Bible teaches that the gifts are
> to continue until Jesus returns.

These parables of Jesus seem to refute the classic view of dispensationalism that sees the end-time Church lukewarm instead of victorious and in revival. As long as there is a baptism in the name of the Father, the Son, and the Holy Spirit, the newly baptized are to be taught to heal the sick and cast out demons. This is part of the New Testament standard for discipleship.

A study of Scripture finds the apostle Paul confirming the teachings of Jesus regarding the continuation of spiritual gifts. In Romans 11:29 Paul explicitly rejects the teaching that spiritual gifts were only temporary and were to end 1) with the death of the apostles, 2) with the death of their immediate disciples, or 3) with the canonization of the Bible.[1] "For God's gifts [Greek: *charismata*] and his call are irrevocable." Another translation, the King James Version, says they are "without repentance," meaning God does not change his mind about giving the gifts and then taking them back.

Cessationists have argued that this passage has been taken out of context and does not apply to the gifts of the Spirit because it deals with Israel's election—not spiritual gifts. Problematically, cessationists have the logic of the passage backward; it is not "the salvation of the Jews" *to which* this principle of continuation is limited—it is the exact opposite. Paul appeals to a separate *universal principle*—the charismata and the calling of God is not withdrawn to show that *a specific case*, the salvation of the Jews, is assured. Dr. Ruthven argues that Romans 11:29 is a paraphrase of Isaiah 59:21, given the context of Isaiah 59:20 in the verse above—very similar to how it is used in the context of "calling" of Jews in Acts 2:38-39.[2]

Other Old Testament Scriptures also refute *dispensational cessationism*, which is an ideology that teaches that God only worked miracles during certain periods of time when He wanted to give revelation about new doctrinal understanding. As Jack Deere has pointed out, this "period theory" actually does not work because there are times when God was working miracles, wonders, healings, and/or signs that were not during the special times that dispensationalists claim.[3] One particular passage that refutes this argument is from the book of Jeremiah.

> *You performed miraculous signs and wonders in Egypt* **and have continued them to this day, both in Israel and among all mankind,** *and have gained the renown that is still yours. You brought your people Israel out of Egypt with signs and wonders, by a mighty hand and an outstretched arm and with great terror* (Jeremiah 32:20-21).

The emphasized passage in this verse gives expression to Jeremiah's statement that the signs and wonders not only occurred during the time of the Exodus but *continued* to his (Jeremiah's) day.

Dispensational cessationism is also refuted in First Corinthians 1:4–8:

> *I thank my God always concerning you for the grace of God which was given you by Christ Jesus, that you were enriched in everything by Him in all utterance and all knowledge, even as the testimony of Christ was confirmed in you, so that you come short in no gift, eagerly waiting for the revelation of our Lord Jesus Christ, who will also confirm you to the end, that you may be blameless in the day of our Lord Jesus Christ* (NKJV).

Here we see the continuation of all the gifts until Jesus Christ is revealed. Paul clearly says that Christians were not to lack *any* gift as they wait for the revelation of Jesus Christ. Crucially important is the promise that "He will continue to confirm (presumably in the same charismatic way—healings, miracles, etc.) to the end" of the age. The Greek word for "confirm" is *bebaioō*, which is used in the New Testament as "miraculous" or "charismatic" revelation-establishing faith.[4]

First Corinthians 13:8–12 is also biblical evidence against the dispensational cessationist position. Interestingly enough, this is only one of the few Scriptures that cessationists use in an attempt to justify their theological position that the gifts would cease *when perfection comes.*

> *Love never fails. But where there are prophecies, they will cease; where there are tongues, they will be stilled; where there is knowledge, it will pass away.*

*For we know in part and we prophesy in part, **but when perfection comes, the imperfect disappears.** When I was a child, I talked like a child, I thought like a child, I reasoned like a child. When I became a man, I put childish ways behind me. Now we see but a poor reflection as in a mirror; then we shall see face to face. Now I know in part; then I shall know fully, even as I am fully known* (1 Corinthians 13:8–12).

Much of the debate is centered around verse 10: "Love never fails. But where there are prophecies, they will cease; where there are tongues, they will be stilled; where there is knowledge, it will pass away. For we know in part and we prophesy in part, but when perfection comes, the imperfect disappears."

The "perfect" is considered by cessationists to be the Bible, whereas non-cessationists consider perfection to be the second coming of Jesus. The second coming of Jesus was the interpretation given by orthodox Catholic patristic fathers. This verse was actually used to confront the Montanists in the second century—an early Charismatic group that ultimately veered off into error and taught that prophecy would end with them[5] because Jesus was coming back in their lifetime. The very Scripture used by cessationists to support their claims was used by the early Church to refute cessationist theory.

We find yet more evidence for the continuation of the gifts in Paul's letter to the Galatians. The churches in Galatia founded by Paul, their spiritual father, experienced miracles. Paul writes in Galatians 3:5, "Does God give you his Spirit and work miracles among you because you observe the law, or because you believe what you heard?" The verb tense Paul uses here is present tense, not past tense, and implies that the miraculous nature of the life of the Church continued even when their apostle (Paul) was not present among them.

It is interesting to note that the NIV emphasizes the phrase "believe what you heard." However, most translations translate the Greek either as "hearing with faith" or, less frequently, "hearing of faith." Yet the notes to the New American Standard Bible as well as Young's Literal Translation state that it should literally be translated as "hearing of faith." The emphasis is on the "hearing of faith," rather than the NIV emphasis, which seems to imply a different process of remembering a verbal message instead of responding to immediate revelation.

In Ephesians chapter 1, Paul makes several distinctions—between the faith with which they have believed the gospel and were saved (verse 13), the faith with which they continue in the Lord (verse 15), and the further operation of the Spirit in his prayers for them (verses 17–23). Paul's constant prayers are for God to "give the Spirit of wisdom and revelation, so that you may know him better" (Eph. 1:17).[6]

> *And you also were included in Christ when you heard the word of truth, the gospel of your salvation. Having believed, you were marked in him with a seal, the promised Holy Spirit, who is a deposit guaranteeing our inheritance until the redemption of those who are God's possession—to the praise of his glory. For this reason, ever since I heard about your faith in the Lord Jesus and your love for all the saints, I have not stopped giving thanks for you, remembering you in my prayers. I keep asking that the God of our Lord Jesus Christ, the glorious Father, may give you the Spirit of wisdom and revelation, so that you*

*may know him better. I pray also that the eyes of your heart may be enlightened in order that you may know the hope to which he has called you, the riches of his glorious inheritance in the saints, and his incomparably great power for us who believe. That power is like the working of his mighty strength, which he exerted in Christ when he raised him from the dead and seated him at his right hand in the heavenly realms, far above all rule and authority, power and dominion, and every title that can be given, not only in the present age but also in the one to come. And God placed all things under his feet and appointed him to be head over everything for the church, which is his body, the fullness of him who fills everything in every way* (Ephesians 1:13–23).

Healings, miracles, signs, and
wonders are the number-one way
God receives glory in Scripture.

Two things are of particular note here. First, the receiving of the Holy Spirit continues until the final redemption of those who are God's possession, the final redemption being the second coming of Christ. Second, the giving of the Spirit is extremely powerful.

Healings, miracles, signs, and wonders are the number-one way God receives glory in Scripture. When one understands that glory and power are synonyms and that the primary way

God receives glory in the Bible is through signs and wonders, miracles and healings,[7] it implies that all the gifts *have* to continue until Jesus returns.

## FIVE-FOLD OFFICE GIFTS OF CHRIST

Ephesians 4:7–13 teaches that the office gifts of apostles, prophets, evangelists, pastors, and teachers are to continue, "until we all reach unity in the faith and in the knowledge of the Son of God and become mature, attaining to the whole measure of the fullness of Christ."

> *But to each one of us grace has been given as Christ apportioned it. This is why it says: "When he ascended on high, he led captives in his train and gave gifts to men." (What does "he ascended" mean except that he also descended to the lower, earthly regions? He who descended is the very one who ascended higher than all the heavens, in order to fill the whole universe.) It was he who gave some to be apostles, some to be prophets, some to be evangelists, and some to be pastors and teachers, to prepare God's people for works of service, so that the body of Christ may be built up until we all reach unity in the faith and in the knowledge of the Son of God and become mature, attaining to the whole measure of the fullness of Christ* (Ephesians 4:7–13).

Having determined what the Scriptures say regarding the duration of these office gifts, a definition of their purpose is possible, which is to "prepare God's people for works of service, so that the body of Christ may be built up."

The Church today is in vital need of these gifts. We can grieve the Holy Spirit by not listening to Him, ignoring Him, and not exercising His "gracelets," which are His grace that comes to us in the gifts of the Spirit. "And do not grieve the Holy Spirit of God, with whom you were sealed for the day of redemption" (Eph. 4:30). Ephesians further urges believers to "be strong in the Lord and in his mighty power."

*Finally, be strong in the Lord and in his mighty power. Put on the full armor of God so that you can take your stand against the devil's schemes. For our struggle is not against flesh and blood, but against the rulers, against the authorities, against the powers of this dark world and against the spiritual forces of evil in the heavenly realms. Therefore put on the full armor of God, so that when the day of evil comes, you may be able to stand your ground, and after you have done everything, to stand. Stand firm then, with the belt of truth buckled around your waist, with the breastplate of righteousness in place, and with your feet fitted with the readiness that comes from the gospel of peace. In addition to all this, take up the shield of faith, with which you can extinguish all the flaming arrows of the evil one. Take the helmet of salvation and the sword of the Spirit, which is the word of God. And pray in the Spirit on all occasions with all kinds of prayers and requests. With this in mind, be alert and always keep on praying for all the saints* (Ephesians 6:10–18).

Paul makes it abundantly clear that in order to engage in victorious spiritual warfare, based on Ephesians 6, the supernatural endowments of the Spirit are absolutely necessary.

Many commentators believe this "praying in the Spirit" may be a reference to praying in unknown tongues. I believe his "mighty power" surely includes the power to heal and the working of miracles.

## FRUIT OF THE SPIRIT, GIFTS OF THE SPIRIT

There is much talk in the Church today that puts the gifts of the Spirit and the fruit of the Spirit at odds. This stems from a misunderstanding of these words, specifically the word *fruit*, and how these words should be examined in their appropriate contexts. You will see that, in some cases, *fruit* refers not only to the characteristics of Christ being formed in our lives, but also the demonstrational power of Christ being released *through* our lives. There is the fruit of the Spirit as identified by Paul in Galatians, which identifies character traits that Christ-followers should exhibit because the Holy Spirit lives inside of them. This is absolutely true and much needed. But there are other kinds of fruit that Paul and Jesus mention.

Philippians 1:9–11 states, "And this is my prayer: that your love may abound more and more in knowledge and depth of insight, so that you may be able to discern what is best and may be pure and blameless until the day of Christ, filled with the fruit of righteousness that comes through Jesus Christ—to the glory and praise of God."

One way of looking at the connection between fruit and glory is to understand that glory equals power, and fruit—as used by Paul in this context—can mean the fruit of John 15, which reveals the inner working of the Spirit that makes believers fruitful. This working of the Spirit begins with love and opens up to more and more "knowledge and depth of insight," as Paul references in this passage from Philippians. This knowledge and insight reveal the purposes of God and enable us to be confident in our prayers, making them more powerful to manifest miracles and healings.

The "fruit of righteousness" means moral fruit and supernatural deeds, especially miracles and healings. These all come by the Spirit. The intimacy, the abounding in insight and depth of knowledge do not refer to insight or depth of knowledge of doctrine or theology, but rather of God Himself. Such knowledge also extends to the awareness of God's immediate directives for that which He wants to do in the immediate present or through upcoming ministry opportunities. As believers learn His ways and discern how to hear His communications, these revelations become the source of their faith to do or produce the "fruits of righteousness."

Two passages make this clear:

> *But as surely as God is faithful, our message to you is not "Yes" and "No." For the Son of God, Jesus Christ, who was preached among you by me and Silas and Timothy, was not "Yes" and "No," but in him it has always been "Yes." For no matter how many promises God has made, they are "Yes" in Christ. And so through him the "Amen" is spoken by us to the glory of God* (2 Corinthians 1:18–21).

> *It is written: "I believed; therefore I have spoken." With that same spirit of faith we also believe and therefore speak* (2 Corinthians 4:13).

Paul is not the only one to declare that the spiritual gifts are to continue. Peter indicates this as well.

*The end of all things is near. Therefore, be clear minded and self-controlled so that you can pray. Above all, love each other deeply, because love covers over a multitude of sins. Offer hospitality to one another without grumbling. Each one should use whatever gift he has received to serve others, faithfully administering God's grace in its various forms. If anyone speaks, he should do it as one speaking the very words of God. If anyone serves, he should do it with the strength God provides, so that in all things God may be praised through Jesus Christ. To him be the glory and the power forever and ever. Amen* (1 Peter 4:7–11).

God's power is meant to shield believers until the salvation that is consummated in the last time. Peter is anticipating the end of time coming soon. In verse 10 he admonishes readers that "each one should use whatever gift he has received to serve others, faithfully administering God's grace in its various forms." Because God's gifts are a form of His grace, the various gifts reflect various forms of grace. Thus, to say that some of the gifts have ended would be tantamount to saying some of God's grace has ended. There is nothing in the text that hints that these forms of God's grace were to end prior to the end of time.

In addition to Jesus, we see that Paul, Peter, and John also have an understanding that the gifts will continue until Jesus returns. In First John 2:26–28, John refers to an anointing from God that is to remain in believers.[8] This "anointing is real and not counterfeit." John encourages believers to continue in Jesus so they will be confident and unashamed before the Lord at His coming. Here we see a direct reference to Jesus' second coming. There is no indication in this text and its context that a time would arise when the believers would no longer need this anointing or that it would be taken away from them.

The New Testament makes a very compelling theological case for the continuation of the present availability of God's supernatural power and gifts. In fact, one needs to read new, external information into the scriptural text in order to build any type of case for the cessation theory that the sign gifts and supernatural enabling of the Spirit have ceased.

# CHAPTER 5

# A THEOLOGY OF HEALING DEMONSTRATION AND EMPOWERMENT

For some Christians, it is not a stretch to endorse a theological paradigm where God heals...*if* He so wills to heal. Typically, those who uphold this ideology will insist that God can do whatever He wants, however He chooses; that healing is divine and sovereign; it is not something that can be commanded or controlled. While there is an element of truth here—that God cannot be controlled—the New Testament introduces us to a challenging picture of faith. It is challenging in that God, in His sovereignty, has decided to impart the Holy Spirit to His people and use them as conduits to release His power in the earth. It is not a matter of whether or not He wants to heal. God still heals and He wants to heal through you and me. It is His will to heal. We must learn how to be His conduits.

## HOW TO RESPOND TO AN ANOINTING FOR HEALING

A full theology of healing should address how we as disciples are to react to the power of God working miracles through us. It is all about humility, and Jesus is the pioneer and our example. If anyone had the right to boast in His miraculous power, it would be God Himself in the person of Jesus. Yet, even Jesus assumed the position of a humble servant, modeling to Christ-followers throughout the generations how we are to respond to His healing anointing. "I tell you the truth, the Son can do nothing by himself; he can do only what he sees his Father doing, because whatever the Father does the Son also does" (John 5:19).

> God, in His sovereignty, has decided to impart
> the Holy Spirit to His people and use them as
> conduits to release His power in the earth.

The apostle Peter truly modeled humility and dependence upon Jesus, and his writings further illuminate our path to discipleship in the ministry of healing. He gave all honor to the name of Jesus Christ for the healings accomplished through his (Peter's) hands. We see this in Peter's early ministry.

> *One day Peter and John were going up to the temple at the time of prayer—at three in the afternoon. Now a man crippled from birth was being carried to the temple gate called Beautiful, where he was put every day to beg from those going into the temple courts. When he saw Peter and John about to enter, he asked them for money. Peter looked straight at him, as did John. Then Peter said, "Look at us!" So the man gave them his attention, expecting to get something*

*from them. Then Peter said, "Silver or gold I do not have, but what I have I give you. In the name of Jesus Christ of Nazareth, walk." Taking him by the right hand, he helped him up, and instantly the man's feet and ankles became strong. He jumped to his feet and began to walk. Then he went with them into the temple courts, walking and jumping, and praising God. When all the people saw him walking and praising God, they recognized him as the same man who used to sit begging at the temple gate called Beautiful, and they were filled with wonder and amazement at what had happened to him* (Acts 3:1–10).

In Peter's answer to the Sanhedrin we see his humility and recognition of the power of the name of Jesus.

*While the beggar held on to Peter and John, all the people were astonished and came running to them in the place called Solomon's Colonnade.* **When Peter saw this, he said to them: "Men of Israel, why does this surprise you? Why do you stare at us as if by our own power or godliness we had made this man walk?** *The God of Abraham, Isaac and Jacob, the God of our fathers, has glorified his servant Jesus. You handed him over to be killed, and you disowned him before Pilate, though he had decided to let him go. You disowned the Holy and Righteous One and asked that a murderer be released to you. You killed the author of life, but God raised him from the dead. We are witnesses of this.* **By faith in the name of Jesus, this man whom you see and know was made strong. It is Jesus' name and the faith that comes through him** *that has given this complete healing to him, as you can all see"* (Acts 3:11–16).

> The anointing and authority to heal the sick
> has nothing to do with the person; rather,
> it has everything to do with the Anointed
> One who works through the person.

Peter knew he performed miracles by the power of the Holy Spirit working in the authority of Jesus' name. "If we are being called to account today for an act of kindness shown to a cripple and are asked how he was healed, then know this, you and all the people of Israel: *It is by the name of Jesus Christ of Nazareth*, whom you crucified but whom God raised from the dead, that this man stands before you healed" (Acts 4:9-10).

The anointing and authority to heal the sick has nothing to do with the person; rather, it has everything to do with the Anointed One who works *through* the person. Peter was able to release healing to the lame beggar because of the authority of Jesus' name and the power of God that flowed through Him. Even though one might label Peter a miracle-worker in this example, the very ability he had to be a catalyst for this miracle came from the indwelling presence of the Holy Spirit.

Peter's example serves to remind us to live in a place of humility, ever recognizing that the authority to heal the sick comes exclusively through the supreme name of Jesus Christ.

# THE MYSTERY OF DIVINE HEALING

Healing often flows through human vessels, and as such there is a great deal of mystery associated with the ministry of healing. One cannot predict *who* will be healed in a meeting and can only estimate *how many* of the people in the meeting will be healed.

Quite often I experience meetings where the numbers of healings in relationship to the total number of attendees reaches 40 percent. Occasionally the percentage reaches 50 to 60 percent, and on rare occasions the percentage reaches 75 percent.

Once, in a meeting of 11,000 people, the percentage healed reached 90 percent. This meeting had a very unusual visitation of the angelic, which was the probable cause for the significantly higher percentage of healings.[1] This particular event occurred in Manaus, Brazil, in a church pastored by Apostle Rene Terre Nova. For the preceding seven to eight nights, the percentage of healings relative to crowd size was 20-30 percent a night.

On the night of angelic visitation, the meeting began with a sighting of warrior angels who later were involved in clearing the heavenlies in the facility. Later in the meeting, hundreds of healing angels were sighted by a "seer." Without mentioning this to the congregation, a declaration was made that "a lot of healings are about to occur over on my right," which was where the angels were sighted. When the seer was asked how he knew these twelve- to eighteen-inch whirlwinds of fire were healing angels, his response was, "I do not know how I know, I just know." The fruit of this night was that 90 percent of the 11,000 attendees indicated they had received a healing in their body. This church has since grown from 40,000 to 70,000 members in one congregation in one city. This inconsistency in the percentages of those healed is a mystery that involves the greater and lesser anointing for healing that is available at different times in the lives of those disciples ministering healing, both then and now.

Anyone involved in healing ministry must recognize that there will be times of greater and lesser degrees of anointing for healing. The gospel accounts depict the various degrees of anointing in the ministry of Jesus for healings and miracles. For example, in the gospel of Luke we find Jesus sitting before the Pharisees and teachers of the law who have come from every village of Galilee and from Judea and Jerusalem. The Scriptures tell us that, "the power of the Lord was present for him to heal the sick" (Luke 5:17). Luke then goes on to tell us the story of the paralytic who is lowered through the ceiling and is healed by Jesus. But in the gospel of Mark we find Jesus unable to perform miracles in His hometown.

> *Jesus left there and went to his hometown, accompanied by his disciples. When the Sabbath came, he began to teach in the synagogue, and many who heard him were amazed. "Where did this man get these things?" they asked. "What's this wisdom that has been given him, that he even does miracles! Isn't this the carpenter? Isn't this Mary's son and the brother of James, Joseph, Judas and Simon? Aren't his sisters here with us?" And they took offense at him. Jesus said to them, "Only in his hometown, among his relatives and in his own house is a prophet without honor." He could not do any miracles there, except lay his hands on a few sick people and heal them. And he was amazed at their lack of faith* (Mark 6:1–6).

Notice how the Luke 5:17 passage implies that Jesus was dependent upon the anointing from God for power to heal, while John 5:19 states it clearly, as does John 5:30. This revelation truly makes Jesus the author and finisher of our faith (see Heb. 12:2) and is consistent with the great kenotic passage of Philippians 2:6–8, which reads, "Who, being in very nature God, did not consider equality with God something to be grasped, but made himself nothing, taking the very nature of a servant, being made in human likeness. And being found in appearance as a man, he humbled himself and became obedient to death—even death on a cross!"

Some have interpreted these passages to mean that though Jesus was God incarnate, He performed His miracles in His humanity—as a man dependent upon the Holy Spirit. The Church dealt with the nature of Jesus at the Council of Chalcedon.[2] The New Testament data indicates that Jesus decided not to utilize His omnipotence, choosing to limit this aspect of His deity during His incarnation. In turn, He worked miracles out of His humanity so that He truly could be the author and finisher of faith.[3] He is not just the redeemer, savior, healer, and baptizer in the Holy Spirit; He is also the model for every believer. Instead of the emphasis of the *moral influence theory of the atonement* that was popular among liberal scholars, what Jesus models for us is based on discipleship—on what is possible through the power of the Holy Spirit. Such a perspective is much more in line with Pentecostal and Charismatic scholarship and is consistent with Jesus' statement in John 14:12, "I tell you the truth, anyone who has faith in me will do [the miraculous works] I have been doing. He will do even greater things than these, because I am going to the Father."

Jesus chose to live dependent upon the anointing of the Holy Spirit to release divine healing, so there were times when that manifestation of power ebbed and flowed, giving us clear examples of when healing power was *available* but not *accessed* because of the lack of faith present (in Jesus' hometown).

Paul's ministry of healing did not always operate at a consistent level of power. He had to leave one of the members of his apostolic team sick in Miletus (see 2 Tim. 4:20). It remains unanswered why Paul, who "did extraordinary miracles" in Ephesus, was not able to bring healing to his friend. There is also the issue of Paul's own illness that was the occasion for his visit to the Galatians. "As you know, it was because of an illness that I first preached the gospel to you. Even though my illness was a trial to you, you did not treat me with contempt or scorn" (Gal. 4:13-14).[4]

We see yet another example of the ebb and flow of power in Paul's healing ministry in his letter to the church in Philippi.

*But I think it is necessary to send back to you Epaphroditus, my brother, fellow worker and fellow soldier, who is also your messenger, whom you sent to take care of my needs. For he longs for all of you and is distressed because you heard he was ill. Indeed he was ill, and almost died. But God had mercy on him, and not on him only but also on me, to spare me sorrow upon sorrow. Therefore I am all the more eager to send him, so that when you see him again you may be glad and I may have less anxiety. Welcome him in the Lord with great joy, and honor men like him, because he almost died for the work of Christ, risking his life to make up for the help you could not give me* (Philippians 2:25-30).

Epaphroditus was so ill that he almost died while in Paul's company, illustrating that not everyone is healed through prayer. What all of this tells us is that healing cannot be accessed via a formula.

## MOTIVATION FOR HEALING

There are many motivations for healing found in Scripture—that the local church will grow, many will come to Christ, the mercy of God will be revealed, and the love of God will be manifested. However, if we examine these more closely we see that there can be a degree of selfish interest in all of these motivations that we must guard against. It is easy to be more excited for *your* church to grow than for other churches, or to be more excited when God reveals His mercy to someone you know than to someone you don't know. While we have an inclination toward earthly motivations, the highest, most pure and unselfish motivation for healing and miracles to occur is so that Jesus' name will be held in high honor.

In Ephesus, Paul stayed for two years and did extraordinary miracles in the name of Jesus (see Acts 19:11, 15, 17b). As a result, the people of Ephesus saw on the one hand the good fruits of ministry in Jesus' name, and on the other hand the devastating results of an attempt to use the name of Jesus in a magical manner by those who were not His followers (see Acts 19:14). The sons of Sceva, who falsely attempted to heal in Jesus' name, were recognized as frauds by the very demonic spirit they were attempting to drive out of a man. Make no mistake, the demonic know the authority of Jesus and so should we.

Our motivation for ministering healing must always be to honor the name of Jesus Christ. This is the highest motivation for healing, and from Scripture we can see that this desire even motivated Jesus. In His upper room discourse, Jesus spoke about his desire to glorify the Father, and the Father's desire to glorify Him. "And I will do whatever you ask in my name, so that the Son may bring glory to the Father" (John 14:13). John 15:8 continues, "This is to my Father's glory, that you bear much fruit, showing yourselves to be my disciples." John 16:14 adds, "He will bring glory to me by taking from what is mine and making it known to you."

> As long as the Holy Spirit is present on the earth, residing in human temples, the plan of God is to authorize anointed vessels to release His healing and deliverance to those in need.

The authority to heal the sick is intended to continue through Christ-followers throughout the centuries. It was never purposed to end with Jesus, the twelve apostles, or even the early Church. As long as the Holy Spirit is present on the earth, residing in human temples, the plan of God is to authorize anointed vessels to release His healing and deliverance to those in need. We must approach healing ministry from a posture of humility, recognizing that it is not about man performing miracles or human names receiving notoriety because of the wonders performed. The great motivation for healing ministry is to see the supremacy and exclusivity of Jesus Christ known throughout the earth.

> *And the glory of the Lord will be revealed, and all mankind together will see it. For the mouth of the Lord has spoken* (Isaiah 40:5).

# CHAPTER 6

# THEOLOGICAL FOUNDATIONS FOR IMPARTATION

For spiritual gifts to be released and activated in the Church today (in a greater degree), we must return to the "elementary teaching" of impartation. According to Scripture, the "laying on of hands" is a basic tenet, but sadly it has been neglected, and as a result we have witnessed a widespread neglect of the graces and gifts that accompany impartation—namely, the demonstration of God's healing power through everyday Christ-followers.

In Brazil, where I have been privileged to minister many times over the years, the best translation of the English word *impartation* is the phrase "transference of the anointing." Even though the term *impartation* is not widely used in the greater Protestant Church today, the fact remains that the practice of impartation is considered by Scripture to be an "elementary teaching." Hebrews 6:1–3 states, "Therefore let us leave the elementary teachings about Christ and go on to maturity, not laying again the foundation of repentance from acts that lead to death, and of faith in God, instruction about baptisms, the laying on of hands, the resurrection of the dead, and eternal judgment. And God permitting, we will do so."

Clearly, the writer of Hebrews was saying in this passage that "the laying on of hands" is to be considered basic to the Christian life—foundational, an "elementary teaching" of the apostolic Church. In both Testaments, the Bible teaches the principle of receiving an "anointing" from God. This anointing may be a gift or gifts of the Spirit, a filling of the Holy Spirit—especially for power—or the baptism in the Holy Spirit. The idea of "impartation" or the "transference of anointing" is clearly a strong biblical concept.

Over the course of many years of ministry I have seen that there is more power, more passion, more purpose, more pleasure in God, and more fruit from the ministry of the Holy Spirit working through believers as a result of the ministry of impartation. In fact, of all the things I value, the ministry of impartation is most important to me. I love seeing people receive healing, deliverance, salvation, and rededication to Jesus. But, I realize that there is a multiplication of healing, deliverance, salvation and rededications through impartation because others begin to be powerfully used in these ways.

## IMPARTATION THOUGH THE LAYING ON OF HANDS

As we consider the biblical examples, we see that anointing often came through the laying on of hands. However, it is important to understand that the laying on of hands is certainly not the only way of receiving an impartation from God. It is simply one of two ways seen in Scripture, the other way being waiting on God through prayer. The laying on of hands for impartation is, however, a means often forgotten and neglected by the Church and therefore important to our study.

My own ministry has been characterized by impartation since God birthed revival in 1994 in Toronto, Canada. Known as the "Toronto Blessing," this mighty outpouring from God, according to modern church history books, represents one of the greatest revival movements of the twentieth century, resulting in the longest protracted meeting in the history of North America. During its first year, the "Blessing" spread to 55,000 churches around the world, with over three million people visiting the church in Toronto during those first few years. Thousands rededicated their lives, were saved and empowered, and were equipped to minister more effectively, often via impartation either sovereignly or through the laying on of hands.

The results of this empowerment and equipping are still ongoing. Thousands of churches have been planted worldwide with millions of new believers coming into the kingdom and healings abounding.[1]

Luke is the historian of the Holy Spirit. His gospel of Luke and record of events in the book of Acts is history written with theological significance and consideration. He recounts in Acts several instances where people are filled with the Holy Spirit *without* the mention of the "laying on of hands."

> *When the day of Pentecost came, they were all together in one place. Suddenly a sound like the blowing of a violent wind came from heaven and filled the whole house where they were sitting. They saw what seemed to be tongues of fire that separated and came to rest on each of them. All of them were filled with the Holy Spirit and began to speak in other tongues as the Spirit enabled them (Acts 2:1–4).*

Acts 4:29–31 continues with, "'Now, Lord, consider their threats and enable your servants to speak your word with great boldness. Stretch out your hand to heal and perform miraculous signs and wonders through the name of your holy servant Jesus.' After they prayed, the place where they were meeting was shaken. And they were all filled with the Holy Spirit and spoke the word of God boldly."

> The Day of Pentecost was not when they first received the Holy Spirit, but the day they were "filled with the Holy Spirit."

Acts 10:44–47 follows with, "While Peter was still speaking these words, the Holy Spirit came on all who heard the message. The circumcised believers who had come with Peter were astonished that the gift of the Holy Spirit had been poured out even on the Gentiles. For they heard them speaking in tongues and praising God. Then Peter said, 'Can anyone keep these people from being baptized with water? They have received the Holy Spirit just as we have.'"

According to the gospel of John, the disciples received the Holy Spirit when Jesus breathed upon them on the evening of the day of His resurrection. Therefore, the Day of Pentecost was not when they first received the Holy Spirit, but the day they were "filled with the Holy Spirit." "Again Jesus said, 'Peace be with you! As the Father has sent me, I am sending you.' And with that he breathed on them and said, 'Receive the Holy Spirit'" (John 20:21-22).

In Acts 2 and 4, the Holy Spirit came upon believers who were looking to God for enabling power. As we saw in the Acts 10:44 passage, as Peter preached for the first time to Gentiles, "the Holy Spirit came on all who heard the message" even as they were being saved through the message.

More pertinent to this study, however, are Luke's accounts where the Holy Spirit or gifts of the Spirit were imparted with the laying on of hands. There is the revival in Samaria:

> *When the apostles in Jerusalem heard that Samaria had accepted the word of God, they sent Peter and John to them. When they arrived, they prayed for them that they might receive the Holy Spirit, because the Holy Spirit had not yet come upon any of them; they had simply been baptized into the name of the Lord Jesus. Then Peter and **John placed their hands on them**, and they received the Holy Spirit* (Acts 8:14–17).

Apparently, the giving of the Holy Spirit was accompanied by some visible manifestation because Luke continues with the reaction of Simon the sorcerer. Acts 8:18-19 reads, "When Simon saw that the Spirit was given at the laying on of the apostle's hands, he offered them money and said, 'Give me also this ability so that everyone on whom I lay my hands may receive the Holy Spirit.'"

A second passage regarding the laying on of hands for impartation is found in Luke's theological-historical account in Acts 19:6. Here Paul, rather than Peter and John, places his hands upon newly baptized believers in Ephesus. Acts 19:6-7 reads, "When Paul placed his hands on them, the Holy Spirit came on them, and they spoke in tongues and prophesied. There were about twelve men in all."

In both these stories, in Samaria and in Ephesus, it is significant that the experience of receiving the Holy Spirit came after the experience of believing. Some teach that the baptism of the Holy Spirit happens at salvation, but one is hard-pressed to prove this from the writings of Luke. It did not happen that way in any of the six passages discussed so far. These are all references from the earliest history of the New Testament Church, dealing with when and how people received the Holy Spirit or indicating what it looked like when the Spirit "came upon" or "filled" believers. The focus of these events is a distinct impartation of the Holy Spirit rather than the regeneration of the Holy Spirit that occurs at salvation.

In Romans, we again find the concept of impartation. This time it is for the impartation of spiritual gifts to the Christians at Rome. Paul says, "I long to see you so that I may impart to you some spiritual gift to make you strong—that is, that you and I may be mutually encouraged by each other's faith" (Rom. 1:11-12).

The activity of the Holy Spirit was vital to Paul's understanding of his role as an apostle. At the end of his letter to the Romans, Paul emphasizes the connection between his proclamation of the word and the empowerment of the Spirit. Romans 15:17–19 states, "Therefore I glory in Christ Jesus in my service to God. I will not venture to speak of anything except what Christ has accomplished through me in leading the Gentiles to obey God by what I have said and done—by the power of signs and miracles, through the power of the Spirit. So from Jerusalem all the way around to Illyricum, I have fully proclaimed the gospel of Christ."

In this passage, Paul seems to understand that the effectiveness of his ministry was not simply the result of what he preached, but of what he *did* as well—the "power of signs and miracles, through the power of the Spirit."

I am indebted to Dr. Gordon Fee who brought to my attention that Paul's most foundational doctrine was the *experience* of the Holy Spirit as the basis for certainty of one's salvation. It is a realization of God's empowering presence in one's life. This was even more foundational for Paul than justification by grace through faith.[2] With such an emphasis upon receiving the empowering presence of God through His Spirit, and the realization that the presence and activity of the Holy Spirit was the true source of his own fruitfulness as a minister of the gospel, it should not surprise us to see Paul wanting to come to the Romans to impart to them some spiritual gift. Nor should it surprise one to see Paul reminding Timothy, his beloved son in the ministry, to "fan into flame the gift of God, which is in you *through the laying on of my hands.*" (2 Tim. 1:6)

For Paul, Timothy, Peter, John, and by logical inference the entire early Christian Church, the impartation of anointing through the laying on of hands was an important catalyst for effective ministry, characterized by the manifest presence of God, and for operating in the complete gifts of the Holy Spirit. It was this first Church—small, despised, and poor — that changed the world in the power of God's Spirit working through them!

God has promised another final and radical outpouring among the nations before His Son returns. Again, He will bring it about through His people. If we are to walk in this high calling (see John 20:21), we cannot forget nor neglect the resources of heaven made available to those who are humble and hungry enough to receive. God is not looking for the well-financed, the well-educated, or even those well experienced in ministry. He is simply looking for those who are willing to yield their hearts and live by all God wants to work through them—those who are willing to believe for more because *there is more!*

## THE CONTINUATION OF IMPARTATION

Almost all denominations have a theological position that rejects the doctrine of laying on of hands in regard to impartation despite Hebrews 6:1-2. This rejection is usually because impartation is often associated with apostles, and most denominations do not accept the continuation of the apostolic office after the second century.

Among those who disagree are scholars Jon Ruthven, Gary Greig, and Craig Keener, who have written in favor of the continuation of the apostolic office.[3] According to Acts 9:17-18, impartation was not reserved to the office of apostle, even in the first century.[4]

Cessationism understands Catholic theology to say that popes are modern-day apostles who can write new doctrine, causing them (cessationists) to reject the possibility of modern-day apostles, thereby protecting the belief in a closed canon and the belief that tradition could not be on the same level of authority as the Bible. However, as Ruthven and others have pointed out, the apostles were not the only writers of the Christian Scriptures. In fact, the majority of apostles never wrote any Scripture.

Because impartation was primarily referenced in the book of Acts as something the apostles were involved in—namely Peter, John, and Paul—it was connected with the work of an apostle. Logically, according to cessationist thinking, if there can be no apostles after the first century, then the laying on of hands for impartation no longer exists as well. Even Pentecostals who believed in the restoration of all gifts and all offices later backed away from the belief in modern apostles.[5]

## IMPARTATION IN THE OLD TESTAMENT

In the Old Testament we find the first reference to the concept of impartation in Numbers 11:16-17. "The Lord said to Moses: 'Bring me seventy of Israel's elders who are known to you as leaders and officials among the people. Have them come to the Tent of Meeting, that they may stand there with you. I will come down and speak with you there, *and I will take of the Spirit that is on you and put the Spirit on them.* They will help you carry the burden of the people so that you will not have to carry it alone.'"

In this passage there is no mention of Moses laying his hands upon the elders, but the concept of transference of anointing from one person to another is clearly present. Equally evident from this text is the principle that impartation, or transference of anointing, is not something man can do, but it is an act of God, totally dependent upon His calling and anointing.

Again, one can see a transference of anointing in Deuteronomy 34:9, "Now Joshua son of Nun was filled with the spirit of wisdom because Moses had laid his hands on him." This time, there is a specific mention of receiving or being filled with the spirit of wisdom when Moses laid hands on Joshua.

Another example can be found in Second Kings 2:9–15, the famous passage that tells of Elijah's anointing being transferred to his spiritual son, Elisha. This passage indicates that it is possible to receive an anointing similar to that of another person. When Elisha begged, "Let me inherit a double portion of your spirit," he was not asking for the power of Elijah's human spirit, but for the Spirit of God to work through him as he (the Spirit) did through his teacher. Likewise, when the people said, "The spirit of Elijah is resting on Elisha," they did not mean that Elisha had received power literally from the spirit of the man, Elijah, but that the Spirit of God was indeed working through Elisha in a powerful way, similar to what they had witnessed in Elijah.

I have seen this same transfer of anointing to my spiritual sons and daughters over the years. Young men like Paul Martini, Will Hart, Ed Roche, Jamie Galloway, and Timothy Berry and many others report that they continually see the impartation and anointing that they received from me transferred to those they pray for in the course of their own ministry, with much fruit for the Kingdom of God resulting.

Examples from the New Testament also reflect two ways to receive power, gifts (including healing and working of miracles), anointing, and fillings or baptisms in the Holy Spirit. One way is through praying and waiting upon God. The other way is through the laying on of hands. Going back to Hebrews 6:1-2, the laying on of hands referred to several things—blessing, identification (see Lev. 16), healing, and *impartation*. Clearly, with or without the actual laying on of hands, the transference of anointing is a biblically documented, God-initiated event.

False ideas continue to be propagated regarding impartation. Such deceptions include notions that God's healing power is *still available,* but is the exclusive property of a healing evangelist or apostolic leader.[6] This kind of thinking implies that the "average" believer is not able to pray for the sick because they do not possess the authority to heal. In this scenario, the strategy is to take the afflicted person to someone who *does* possess such healing authority. While there are obviously men and women, both living today and throughout history, who flow in an unusual healing anointing, this does not discount the privilege of every single Christian filled with the Holy Spirit to lay their hands on the sick and release healing. It is not a ministry office or a title that authorizes us to heal the sick. We are authorized to heal the sick through the name of Jesus Christ and the power of the Holy Spirit dwelling within us.

I once had an impartation service for about 6,000 people in the church. A few years later the senior pastor, an apostolic leader who pastors a church of 30,000 and oversees a network of hundreds of churches with over 300,000 constituents, said to me, "Do you see that woman over there? We call her the "little Randy Clark" because she received the strongest impartation during your ministry time, more than anyone else in our church. She isn't a pastor, she isn't even a cell group leader, but she sees more people healed than anyone else in our church. She sees more people touched by the power when she prays than anyone else in our church, and she sees more people fall under the power of God when she prays than anyone else in our church."

When I hear testimonies like this one I am reminded again why we shouldn't limit the ministry team to elders in the church. There are people who do not have the qualifications to be an elder but who have been anointed by the Holy Spirit with gifts of words of knowledge and gifts of healing and we must allow them to flow in these gifts for the benefit of the body of Christ.

I believe that the Kingdom of God will continue to be powerfully impacted by ministering a fresh impartation of the Spirit to pastors, leaders, and their people, thereby creating a ripple effect so that eventually every nation will be reached by the Kingdom and experience the Father's healing power and love.

If you feel a stirring in your heart for more of the authority of God in your life, allow this prayer for impartation to come upon you now in the power of the Holy Spirit:

> *Lord, create a hunger in me now for the "more" of impartation of your Spirit and your gifts. Create faith in me now to receive gifts through impartation, to receive a new and possibly stronger "filling" of your Spirit through an impartation. I ask this in the power and authority of Jesus' name. Amen.*

# PART THREE

# THE ISSUE OF FAITH IN HEALING

# CHAPTER 7

# HOW TO FLOW IN GOD'S SUPERNATURAL HEALING POWER

## UNDERSTANDING THE NATURE OF FAITH

With a firm biblical foundation for the legitimacy of healing and a knowledge of the availability of healing power for the believer—combined with an understanding that God intends the spiritual gifts to continue—it is time to explore how healing is typically appropriated. In other words, how do we flow in God's supernatural healing power?

Even though I believe Scripture makes clear cases for certain principles and methods, we also see examples where Jesus actually overrides a principle—not principles of morality, ethics, or character, but methods of demonstrating healing and miracles. Although faith is the key and primary way healing is received and demonstrated, God is sovereign and able to perform miracles outside of our structural confines.

With these things in mind, how are we to understand the nature of faith? Is it faith *in* God or is it the faith *of* God? This distinction is important to our understanding of the role of faith in the ministry of healing. Let's begin with Mark 11:22,

"Have faith in God." The Greek (Εχετε πιστιν θεου) has been translated primarily in two ways—as "have faith *in* God" and as "have faith *of* God."[1]

> Although faith is the key and primary way healing is received and demonstrated, God is sovereign and able to perform miracles outside of our structural confines.

Although more translations say "have faith *in* God," there is biblical reason to believe that "have the faith *of* God"[2] may be the better translation, especially in light of the fact that faith is a gift of the Holy Spirit that is mentioned by Paul in First Corinthians 12:9. This gift of faith may be related to the mountain-moving faith mentioned by Jesus. Because the verb "to have" in Mark 11:22 is in the Greek present imperative form, it is a command.

To "have" something is a stative situation—a state of being or an event, rather than an action or active situation. We either have something, or we don't have it. In most languages, we cannot be commanded to assume a stative situation, such as having or possessing an object, but we can be commanded to exercise a voluntary action[3]—for example, *taking hold of* something or *acquiring* something—that will then lead to the stative situation of *having* something.

Typically, when verbs denote stative situations, they do not take the imperative (command) form. One can only be commanded to do what one can voluntarily choose to do. Thus in most languages, including Greek, only verbs denoting voluntary actions occur in the imperative (command) forms. This is why in Mark 11:22 the imperative form of the Greek verb *echein* "to have" requires a translation with the voluntary, active connotation of the verb meaning "to take hold of (something), seize, grip."[4]

Thus, Jesus is commanding His disciples to make an effort to *acquire, take hold of,* or *to seize* the faith of God, which suggests acquiring the faith that *comes from* God.[5] The content of this faith that we are to acquire from God involves receiving divine revelation and hearing God's voice.

Jesus associates faith and hearing God's voice with being Abraham's children (see John 8:39–47; also see Romans 4:11-12: "he [Abraham] is the father of all who believe"; Galatians 3:7: "those who believe are the children of Abraham"). And the pattern of Abraham's faith described in Genesis chapters 12 to 25 clearly consists of hearing the Lord's voice, believing, and obeying Him even when it was risky, dangerous, and difficult to do so (see Gen. 12:1,4; 15:4–6,9–10,23; 21:9–14; 22:2–3).[6]

Regardless of whether we translate certain passages as "have faith *in* God" or "have faith *of* God," what we are talking about is a faith that has its source in God, not in the person praying. It is different from "saving faith," yet even saving faith is a gift of prevenient grace,[7] enabling us to believe the gospel. Rather, this mountain-moving faith is not normal faith that is in some way related to the faithfulness of God as understood by the person praying. Instead, it is a gift of grace, enabling one to believe or have faith for a specific outcome in a specific moment.

## MOUNTAIN-MOVING FAITH

Mountain-moving faith as Jesus defines it in the gospels is a manifestation of a grace gift of faith that comes from God the Holy Spirit. There are three key passages in Scripture that mention mountain-moving faith. One is found in Matthew 21:21-22: "Jesus replied, 'I tell you the truth, if you have faith and do not doubt, not only can you do what was done to the fig tree, but also you can say to this mountain, "Go, throw yourself into the sea," and it will be done. If you believe, you will receive whatever you ask for in prayer.'"

The second is in Mark 11:22-24: "'Have faith in God,' Jesus answered, 'I tell you the truth, if anyone says to this mountain, "Go, throw yourself into the sea," and does not doubt in his heart but believes that what he says will happen, it will be done for him. Therefore I tell you, whatever you ask for in prayer, believe that you have received it, and it will be yours.'" Again, I want to emphasize that this Scripture could grammatically be translated, "Have faith of God" instead of "Have faith in God." In these passages, Jesus is speaking of prevenient grace. Charles Wesley describes it thus, "the divine love that surrounds all humanity and precedes any and all of our conscious impulses. This grace prompts our first wish to please God, our first glimmer of understanding concerning God's will, and our 'first slight transient conviction' of having sinned against God. God's grace also awakens in us an earnest longing for deliverance from sin and death and moves us toward repentance and faith."[8]

The second- and fifth-century interpretation of this text as *of God* instead of *in God* is defined by the remarks of Jacob Arminius: "Concerning grace and free will, this is what I teach according to the Scriptures and orthodox consent: Free will is unable to begin or to perfect any true and spiritual good, without grace.... This grace [*prævenit*] goes before, accompanies, and follows; it excites, assists, operates that we will, and cooperates lest we will in vain."[9]

Apart from God's grace, no one comes to God. In our natural state, as sinners, it is the prevenient grace of God that brings us to that place where we can either receive what is offered to us through the cross and the gospel or reject it. The choice is ours; the grace is God's.

The third is in Matthew 17:20; "He replied, 'Because you have so little faith. I tell you the truth, if you have faith as small as a mustard seed, you can say to this mountain, "Move from here to there" and it will move. Nothing will be impossible for you.'"

The apostle Paul refers to this kind of mountain-moving faith in First Corinthians 12 and 13, where he offers a list of the gifts of the Spirit in chapter 12, and then in chapter 13 gives the motivation for the exercise of these spiritual gifts, which is love. Paul's teaching in chapter 13 is not meant to be an option in opposition to the exercise of the gifts, as if the fruit of love is better than the gift of faith. Instead, he is indicating that the more excellent way is to operate in the gift of faith *motivated* by God's love. Notice that Paul identifies the gift of faith in verse 9.

*Now there are varieties of gifts, but the same Spirit. And there are varieties of ministries, and the same Lord. And there are varieties of effects, but the same God who works all things in all persons. But to each one is given the manifestation of the Spirit for the common good. For to one is given the word of wisdom through the Spirit, and to another the word of knowledge according to the same Spirit; to another faith by the same Spirit, and to another gifts of healing by the one Spirit, and to another the effecting of miracles, and to another prophecy, and to another the distinguishing of spirits, to another various kinds of tongues, and to another the interpretation of tongues. But one and the same Spirit works all these things, distributing to each one individually just as He wills* (1 Corinthians 12:4–11 NASB).

When Paul moves to a discussion of the more excellent way, he again picks up many of the gifts he listed in chapter 12, including faith. He writes in First Corinthians 13:1-2, "If I speak in the tongues of men and of angels, but have not love, I am only a resounding gong or a clanging cymbal. If I have the gift of prophecy and can fathom all mysteries and all knowledge, and if I have a faith that can move mountains, but have not love, I am nothing."

Clearly this faith Paul is referring to is the same faith he wrote about in chapter 12. It is not the normal faith of trusting Jesus for salvation; neither is it referring to "the faith" as a designation for the Christian religion. Likewise, Paul is not referring to the "measure of faith" that he mentions in Romans 12:3, "For by the grace given me I say to every one of you: Do not think of yourself more highly than you ought, but rather think of yourself with sober judgment, in accordance with the measure of faith God has given you."

Instead, this faith Paul is referring to is the faith that is related to the operation of healings and miracles, signs and wonders. It is not faith generated by the human psychic or our ability to "work it up" or confess it into reality. Rather, this faith comes as a gift of grace. In this context, grace should be understood as a divine enablement more so than undeserved favor or forgiveness.

Because of the clear distinction of faith as a gift of grace that brings empowerment for miracles, it seems appropriate to conjecture that the mountain-moving faith Jesus referred to in the gospels is this kind of faith—a manifestation of a grace gift of faith that comes from God the Holy Spirit. This is the emphasis of Dr. Charles Price who was a powerful healing minister in the first half of the twentieth century.[10] This kind of faith produces miracles, and it comes from God as a gift—not the kind of gift that is maintained or is constituted, but a situational gift for the moment. Bishop David Pytches says of this kind of faith: "This gift is a supernatural surge of confidence from the Spirit of God which arises within a person faced with a specific situation or need whereby that person receives a transrational certainty and assurance that God is about to act through a word or action."[11]

## VISIONS OF LIGHT

Omar Cabrera spoke of this kind of faith and its supernatural operation as being created by a light that he would see over a person. When he saw this light appear, he knew that the person under the light would receive a miracle.[12]

Similarly, healing evangelist William Branham would see light over people. Both men believed the light was an angel, and where the light was, that was where the miracle would take place. Sometimes for Branham the faith for the miraculous was created by having a vision beforehand, and then he would find himself exactly in the context of the vision. Thus, he knew what to do (how to minister), having seen the scenario played out earlier in a vision.[13]

> When a declaration is spoken—of what
> we believe God intends to do in a given
> situation—faith is released into that situation.

## SPEAKING WORDS OF FAITH

We know faith as a gift of grace, a divine enablement, and one of the ways in which God releases His healing; however, He also releases his healing through spoken words of faith. "Spoken words of faith" can come as declarations, which are different from words of knowledge, prophecies, and testimonies. When a declaration is spoken—of what we believe God intends to do in a given situation—faith is released into that situation. I see this happen again and again in my meetings. It is important to understand that these kinds of declarations come from revelation from the Holy Spirit. They are not something we think up or want to see happen. This is where a distinction is made between faith as an expectation based upon the faithfulness of God, and the faith that is a gift resulting not in confident expectation but in a certainty that God is about to heal or perform a miracle. I have a testimony of this in the section titled "Gifts of Healing" found later in this chapter.

There are several New Testament passages that deal, in a larger context, with the relationship between speaking declarations and faith. In Second Corinthians 1:18–20, we find Paul accused of being unfaithful to his word when he did not come to Corinth as planned. Paul explains that although he did not come as promised, that does not mean that the word of God is unfaithful. The gospel is not *yes* or *no,* says Paul, but all the promises are always *yes* in Christ, and believers should strive to agree with a congregational *amen,* to the glory of God.

In my meetings, when attendees realize that the *amen* is to a specific promise—such as a declaration or a word of knowledge that is a *rhema* word or *logos* word from the Holy Spirit—it is important they speak the *amen* in their hearts, even if the revelatory word is not for them, because we are one body and should be of one accord. It is the response of faith represented in the heartfelt *amen* that releases the power of God for healings and miracles, which in turn brings glory to God.

In Second Corinthians 4, Paul and the apostles are suffering for the gospel, yet he says, "It is written: 'I believed; therefore I have spoken.' With that same spirit of faith we also believe and therefore speak" (2 Cor. 4:13). In his affliction he identifies with David, the psalmist (see Ps. 116:10), as he, like David, expresses his faith in the midst of his affliction. Paul goes on to point to his confidence and hope in the resurrection (see 2 Cor. 4:14), and also in the growing apostolic work of evangelizing more people, which, in turn, causes thanksgiving to overflow to the glory of God (see verse 15).

We have to wonder, as Paul does not finish the quote from David, perhaps he did not intend to limit his thinking to affliction but wanted to expand it to speaking in faith in a more general sense, rather than limiting faithfulness to the faith we have during suffering.

> Because God is the same yesterday, today, and tomorrow, what He has done before He can do again, and it is testimony that sustains this truth.

In Revelation 19:10 we find an angel addressing John's desire to fall at his (the angel's) feet and worship him: "Do not do it! I am a fellow servant with you and with your brothers who hold to the testimony of Jesus. Worship God! For the testimony of Jesus is the spirit of prophecy." In the Old Testament there was the word of God and the testimony of God. Bill Johnson first pointed out that when the people of God forgot the testimony of God, they began to backslide. This "testimony of God" consisted of the mighty deeds God had done among them. Likewise, the testimony of Jesus consists of His mighty deeds, and it is this testimony that releases prophecy. Bill also notes that prophecy carries an invitation to those who hear it to come taste and see that God is good and His mercy is available for all. Because God is the same yesterday, today, and tomorrow, what He has done before He can do again, and it is testimony that sustains this truth. The very word used for testimony in the Hebrew Old Testament (*edut*) has the sense in its root to "repeat or do again." We have the understanding that what God has done for one person He will do again for someone else because He doesn't respect one person above another.

We get a strong sense from the way the term *testimonies* is used in Psalm 119 that focusing on these accounts teaches us the very heart of God for His children (see, for example, verses 24 and 99 in the NASB).

## REVELATORY GIFTS

Pastor John Wimber, founder of the Vineyard Christian Fellowship, and Omar Cabrera, pastor of the Vision of the Future denomination in Argentina, were most instrumental in helping me discover the ways of God regarding revelatory gifts.[14] It was from John Wimber that I learned how to recognize words of knowledge. Between 1984 and 1985 I was able to shadow John in his meeting in the U.S., where I learned how to recognize signs of God's presence. Omar Cabrera taught me the importance of the role of the angelic realm in healing and the importance of asking God to send His angels into meetings. From Omar I learned how the angelic would manifest (to Omar) and how he knew how to interpret what he saw, which created the faith in him for the greatest miracles of his crusades.

From these two men I also learned how to instruct crowds in order to build their faith by teaching on the relationship between gifts of revelation and gifts of power. The gifts of revelation being words of knowledge, words of wisdom, and discerning of spirits; and the gifts of power being healings, faith, and working of miracles. There are also the gifts of speech—tongues, interpretation of tongues, and prophecy. Note that prophecy is a gift of revelation, while also being a gift of speech. Although this simple division of the nine gifts into three sets of three is an oversimplification, it helps when time is limited and it is necessary to teach large crowds about the relationship between revelation and power gifts.

During my forty-five years of ministering to hundreds of thousands of people in thousands of meetings and thirty years of actively praying for the sick, I have noticed the connection between healing and faith and between faith and revelatory gifts. With few exceptions, most miraculous healings involve a gift of faith, and almost always this gift of faith is the result of a revelatory gift. Even when it seemed no gift such as a word of knowledge or a prophecy occurred, there was the *still small voice* of God or an impression from God instructing the person praying as to what to do. The person may not have believed in words of knowledge or understood he or she was having a word of knowledge, when in fact impression is one of the ways words of knowledge occur and one of the ways prophecy occurs.

Once, in Tucson, Arizona, I witnessed a woman healed of paranoid schizophrenia, severe obsessive-compulsive disorder, and anorexia even though there was no word of knowledge for her condition. Her stepfather received an impression from God to go and get her and bring her to our meeting. He did so, and as she sat in the meeting, her healing began. Later that night, at home, she received an impression to anoint her head with oil, which she did. This was followed by a second impression, which instructed her to anoint her whole body with oil. When she obeyed, the *energia* of God knocked her to the floor where she lay all night with currents of electricity going through her body. In the morning she was healed.

On another occasion, in Goiania, Brazil at the Igreja Videira church pastored by Aloisio Silva, a man who was totally blind after having muriatic acid spilled in his eyes fifty years before came to our service for healing. He had no visible pupils or corneas; all that could be seen was thick scar tissue, about an eighth of an inch thick. This man was healed when a woman on our ministry team had an impression to pray for him. So strong was the impression that she prayed for five hours, even though nothing was happening. She kept hearing the words (which came to her as an impression), "Do not stop praying." When she finally did stop, after five hours, in order to catch the bus back to the hotel where the team was staying, there was no change in the man's condition. Three days later the man woke up without scar tissue. New pupils and corneas had formed in his eyes and good vision was restored.

It is important to note that even though there was no specific word of knowledge spoken for either of these people, those involved in their healing were given revelation of what to do through an impression. Although from what I have seen in my years of ministry this is not the norm, it is important to remember that God does not operate within our formulas.

## GIFTS OF HEALING

Oftentimes, gifts of healing will be activated through faith. I have seen this happen many times. Once, in Uberlândia, Brazil a woman was healed of stage four terminal cancer through a gift of healing. It happened this way—her friend had an unusual dream in which she was told that when she met the man whose name was on the opposite side of the coin she had been handed, her friend would be healed of cancer. In the dream, when she turned the coin over, it had the name Randy Clark on it. Both these women were Portuguese speakers and had never heard of my ministry or me. The name Randy Clark is not common to Portuguese and is very rare.

A few days later while driving through the city, she saw a flyer with the name *Randy Clark* on it announcing a meeting for healing. This woman brought her sick friend to the meeting. She was very ill, with just weeks to live. Her friend was able to share her dream with me, and when she did it created a gift of faith in me.

I was so confident the woman would be healed of cancer that even though there were no indications of anything happening when we prayed for her, I persevered in prayer for at least twenty minutes. It was at that point that we saw the first indication of the power of God beginning to touch her. When the fullness of God's power touched her, she began to tremble and shake so hard that she started to bounce in her seat. All the organs in her abdominal cavity were full of cancer, and the bones in her thighs were full of cancer as well. As the power of God went through her body, the heat in her legs became so intense that perspiration began to soak her pant legs.

The heat and power would be upon her for about fifteen to twenty minutes, then it would be gone for about five minutes, then the cycle would repeat as if God were giving her time to rest between waves of healing. She experienced six cycles of heat and power for healing that night and was powerfully healed. Her friend's vision of the coin with my name on it created a persevering faith in me that caused me to pray relentlessly until I saw God's healing power touch her. A gift of healing was activated through my faith.

This kind of faith that comes from God as a gift cannot be attained and is not constant. It cannot be created by the confession of someone or some spiritual exercise. It is simply given by God as a gift. Sometimes the gift comes by revelation of what God intends to do; other times it just comes as its own gift, supplying unnatural faith to "move mountains."

# RELATIONSHIP BETWEEN GRACE, GIFT, AND FAITH

I have seen many healings, scores of thousands of healings, but probably less than 200 miracles in my life thus far. In every miracle, it seemed a gift of faith was present—the type of mountain-moving faith that comes as gift.

In the Scriptures we see what can be termed "degrees" of faith. Jesus seemed to indicate this when he compared the faith of the centurion, who had greater faith than all Israel (see Matt. 8). Jesus' statement about the "little faith" of the disciples suggests this as well (see Matt. 17).[15] God's faith comes from God's grace, and for us this grace is dependent upon a relationship with Jesus—by abiding in Him. Dr. Jim B. McClure addresses this concept of the grace of divine enablement in his book *Grace Revisited*,[16] defining it as both divine authority and dynamic power.

As noted previously, this faith for miracles, even healing, is not constant. It is not constituted; it is situational, as John Wimber so powerfully taught,[17] and there is the connection between grace, gift, and faith as we noted in Romans 12:3, 6.

Rudolf Bultmann, in his article on faith in *The Dictionary of the New Testament*, gives a limited understanding of faith. He notes that faith has multiple meanings including dependence upon, trust in, obedience to, expectation of, and certainty of the Triune God.[18] However, we must turn from word studies if we are to find information about the relationship of faith to miracles and to learn more about the nature of faith. We are not talking about the faith of coming to Christ, but the meaning of faith once someone has come to Christ—in particular, the place of faith in fulfilling the gospel of the Kingdom of

God. Two good sources for a study of this subject are the works of Jon Ruthven and Gary Greig.[19]

The New Covenant is to enable God's followers to hear directly from Him via the Holy Spirit. And because we can hear from God, this hearing produces faith, which results in the mighty works of God.[20] The problem is not the ability of a Christian to hear, but the ability to recognize that what we are hearing (through various means of perception) is from God.[21] In light of the importance of hearing or perceiving, let us consider the importance of the *rhema* of God.

## RHEMA AND LOGOS

The words *rhema* and *logos* are about communication—a word spoken from someone to someone. Although there has been much made of a distinction between *rhema* and *logos* in Charismatic circles, there is not good support for the differentiation.[22] *Logos* often refers to the expression of a thought, a message, or a discourse, whereas *rhema* often refers to that which is said or spoken, an utterance. Though the meanings of these two words overlap in the Greek New Testament, we can contrast them this way—*logos* is the message; *rhema* is the communication of the message. Regardless of whether the word *logos* or *rhema* is used in referring to divine revelation in the New Testament, the connection is very strong between hearing and receiving revelation from God that results in faith.

A word from God allows us to know the specific will of God in a specific situation, thereby causing great faith for answered prayer for a miracle or healing. *Rhema* is the word used for faith in Romans, "But what does it say? 'The word is near you; it is in your mouth and in your heart,' that is, the word of faith we are proclaiming" (Rom. 10:8).

These "words" are often called a prophecy or a word of knowledge in Charismatic, Pentecostal, and Third-wave churches. The more traditional Reformed traditions likely do not use such terms, preferring instead to speak of illumination from God, or, as in the Baptist church my grandmother attended, the description used for such communication was, "the Lord told me" or "the Lord led me."

These revelatory gifts flow out of relationship as Jesus points out in His upper room discourse,[23] and though they are gifts not merited, they happen more often to people who expect them, who understand how to recognize them, and who make a point to pay attention and listen for them.

Faith is also given or created when we experience the faithfulness of God in a particular area of healing. In other words, as we experience healing in a particular area, faith for that area increases. Over time, as more healings occur we develop a stronger faith in that area because we have seen God heal with regularity. For example, because I have regularly seen God heal people with chronic pain or loss of mobility due to surgeries, my faith for this type of healing has increased to the point where I pray at least once in every series of meetings for this particular issue.

## WORDS OF KNOWLEDGE

In my meetings and conferences over the years, I (and many others) have received many words of knowledge that God has used to release faith for healing. Years ago, while conducting a seminar on healing in a church, I met a lady in her seventies. She was facing an operation on her carotid artery to prevent a stroke. The day before the meeting my carotid artery began to jerk and spasm for no apparent reason. Instantly the woman's condition came to mind, and I received faith for her to be healed. My faith was dependent upon this experience, which I perceived to be a word of knowledge.

On the way to the meeting, my carotid artery began to spasm again. My faith rose, and I told everyone in the car that this woman was going to be healed. When we arrived at the church and this dear lady came into the sanctuary, I immediately told her she was going to be healed today. Then I took her by the hand to the front of the church and told the congregation, "Watch what God does; He is going to heal her!" Instantly, as prayer was spoken for her healing, we could see the power of God touching her physically. We learned later that she was healed.

When someone receives a word of knowledge for their condition that causes faith to rise for their healing, a "faith gift" is in operation. This "faith gift word of knowledge" can increase the faith of the one who hears the word and the one who receives it for their healing. For example, in August 2011, I went to minister in a church in Springfield, Ohio. Present that day was a twenty-four-year veteran of the Marine Corps who was very skeptical of healing. Words of knowledge were called out for several of his problems, including sciatica in the right hip, wrists, hands, and shoulder. All of these were locations of pain and limited mobility for him, yet because of his skepticism he never stood up for any of these words of knowledge when they were called out.

As he sat in his seat, heat started coming into his shoulder, and he couldn't ignore it because it was quite strong. It was this physical manifestation of heat that finally caused him to try and move his painful joints and limbs to see if he was being healed. And he was! He was healed of all pain and loss of mobility and of severe fibromyalgia. His faith increased as a result of this, and so did mine.[24]

## UNUSUAL SIGNS: RAISING THE DEAD

The biblical mandate to raise the dead is being followed by believers today, yet skepticism surrounds this type of healing miracle. Although I have not personally had the privilege of being used by God to raise the dead, I have talked to people who have, and I find their testimonies to be entirely credible.

Sometimes the faith to raise the dead is supplied by signs to the one praying. In Mozambique, a key leader in Iris Ministries, Mr. Tanueque, and his wife have been used several times to raise the dead. When interviewed, they indicated that they had been used to raise four people from the dead, and a brother-in-law had been used to raise seven people from the dead. When asked, "How do you know who to pray for? Do you pray for all the dead?" Mr. Tanueque responded, "Of course not; it would be an embarrassment to the church to pray for all the dead. I place my hand on the dead person's foot or near the ankle, and if the place I am touching begins to grow warm, or if while praying for the person under my breath, while my wife is talking to the family, I feel a large bolt of energy go through my body, then I give my wife a sign and she announces, 'We are going to pray for so-and-so to be raised from the dead.' When we do this we see people raised from the dead."

## LAYING THE FOUNDATION

The importance of laying a foundation for healing cannot be overemphasized. It is a key element in the process of ministering healing. The types of healings that are discussed in a meeting will usually lead to more healings of that type occurring. For example, if you share testimonies of people who have been healed of cancer, the faith level of those with cancer will rise and you will typically see a significant increase in those healed of cancer. In my meetings I use both video testimonies and bring people up on stage to testify of their healing. In addition, as the Holy Spirit leads I will verbally put forth an expectation (declaration) for faith. This is usually something as simple as saying, "I believe God is telling me that many will be healed of metal tonight." You will remember in the gospels that people came to Jesus for healing because they had heard the testimony of others who were healed, either directly or indirectly. Their level of faith and expectancy for healing was high as a result.

Often, before I present a healing testimony, either via video or someone sharing, I will tell the people that they can expect healing while listening to the testimony. When I do this, we see more healings. When I don't, usually no one is healed. What this indicates is that healings can come by the sovereignty of God *and* the expectation of those seeking healing. I do believe the lack of healing due to God's sovereignty has been greatly overemphasized, and there has been a great underemphasis on our need to have faith or expectation for healing, especially the dimension of faith that is related to and created by revelatory gifts. This doesn't put all the emphasis upon the people to somehow be able to work up faith, but to understand the ways of God and in so doing have faith created as a gift from God.

In like manner, this applies to words of knowledge. If words of knowledge are given without first laying a foundation of understanding that they reveal the will of God in a particular situation and that people can be healed by simply hearing a word of knowledge without anyone praying for them, then fewer people are healed. However, if time is taken to explain the purpose of words of knowledge—that it is God's will to heal by the word—then many more are healed.

It was an experience in Buenos Aires, Argentina that changed my understanding of words of knowledge and healing, thus changing the way I have ministered ever since. I was ministering as usual, giving words of knowledge, which I intended to follow with prayer for healing, after which I would ask people to stand and wave their hands over their heads if they were 80 percent or more healed. However, when I would give words of knowledge, people would immediately stand and begin waving their hands over their heads, before I had a chance to pray. This happened three times. I kept telling the translator that the people were misunderstanding me until he finally told me that I was the one misunderstanding. Their church was built upon the healing gift of Omar Cabrera and his gift of words of knowledge. These people understood words of knowledge and their purpose and had faith for healing without prayer. They were being healed just by hearing words of knowledge.

This experience changed my ministry and Global Awakening's ministry. Upon returning home to the United States, in my first meeting in North Carolina I shared what had happened in Argentina—how greater expectation brought greater healing. Since that night I never fail to share this, and we typically see many people healed by a word of knowledge before prayer is offered for healing. It was not the sovereignty of God or the nature of disease that changed, but the expectation (faith) of the people. It is important to note that prior to this experience in Argentina I had not seen people healed without prayer for twenty-nine years of ministry, but since that experience I have seen it happen almost every time in every meeting for the past sixteen years.

The nature of faith can seem complex, but the mandate to heal is straightforward. God is intentional about healing, and He is calling us to partner with Him with the same intentionality.

> *At the hands of the apostles many signs and wonders were taking place among the people; and they were all with one accord* (Acts 5:12 NASB).

# CHAPTER 8

# GOD INTENDS TO HEAL

God is intentional about healing, and He will act in ways that express His intentionality. In 2013 I was ministering at Abba's House, a large Southern Baptist church in Hixson, Tennessee. I had already determined that I was going to pray for healing from implanted material and I shared this with the congregation. This congregation had experienced the highest percentage of people healed of complications from surgeries involving implanted materials in the United States that I knew of to date, with 47 percent of those with pain and range of motion restrictions from surgeries healed.[1] Interestingly, prior to mentioning prayer for healing for people with pain and range of motion restrictions from surgery, a young woman, who had had facial reconstruction involving three plates, had a screw in her jawbone that protruded from her gum on the inside of her mouth. She was scheduled to have surgery to remove the screw, but the surgery never happened because, during the meeting, she came forward weeping with the screw in her hand. It had come out of her jawbone. God had healed her.

While this young woman gave her testimony, another man in the congregation started waving his arms wildly. He came forward and testified that he could barely move his right arm due to a break requiring seventeen screws between his shoulder and elbow. He now had complete mobility in every way. There had not been any ministry for metal when these two healings happened. What was happening was in essence a divine setup that built tremendous faith for healing in the meeting, especially for those with implanted materials.[2] God illustrated His power to heal through these two sovereign healings, and we had the wisdom to recognize this was a "way of God,"[3] a sign of His intentionality. Ministry for others with implanted materials immediately followed these two testimonies, and there were twenty-two people who were healed. Forty-seven percent of them had complications from surgeries involving implanted materials.

In contrast to the meeting in Tennessee, there was a meeting I conducted in West Chester, Pennsylvania where we saw the lowest percentage of healings involving complications from surgeries with implanted materials. What was the difference? I believe the difference was due to a difference in the sovereign dimension of God that builds faith in those in attendance.

## REMEMBERING HIS MIGHTY DEEDS

We serve a mighty and glorious God who desires that we draw near to Him and learn His ways, and the surest path to learning His ways begins by studying His mighty deeds as found in the Scriptures. It is here that we find the strong connection between an intimate knowledge of God's ways and His glory. The Psalms in particular speak of God's glory.

> *One generation shall laud your works to another, and shall declare your **mighty acts**...all your faithful shall bless you. They shall speak of the **glory** of your kingdom, and tell of your **power**, to make known to*

*all people your **mighty deeds*** (Psalm 145:4,10–12 NRSV).

*I will come praising the **mighty deeds** of the Lord God, I will praise your righteousness, yours alone. O God, from my youth you have taught me, and I still proclaim your **wondrous deeds**. So even to old age and gray hairs, O God, do not forsake me, until I proclaim your might to all the generations to come. Your **power** and your righteousness, O God, reach the high heavens. You who have done **great things**, O God, who is like you?* (Psalm 71:16–19 NRSV)

*We will not hide them from their children; we will tell to the coming generation the **glorious deeds** of the Lord, and his **might**, and the **wonders** that he has done. He established a decree in Jacob, and appointed a law in Israel, which he commanded our ancestors to teach to their children; that the next generation might know them, the children yet unborn, and rise up and tell them to their children, **so that they should set their hope in God, and not forget the works** of God...and that they should not be like their ancestors...whose spirit was not faithful to God. ...**They forgot what he had done, and the miracles that he had shown them*** (Psalm 78:4–8,11 NRSV).

*I will meditate on **all your work**, and muse on your **mighty deeds**. Your way, O God, is holy. What god is so great as our God? You are the God who **works wonders**; you have displayed **your might** among the peoples. With your **strong arm** you redeemed your people* (Psalm 77:12–15 NRSV).

*O give thanks to the Lord, call on his name, make known his **deeds** among the peoples. Sing to him, sing praises to him; tell of **all his wonderful works**. Glory in his holy name; let the hearts of those who seek the Lord rejoice. Seek the Lord and **his strength**; seek his presence continually. Remember the **wonderful works** he has done, **his miracles*** (Psalm 105:1–5 NRSV).

Perhaps these Psalms give us insight into how the word *testimony* is used in Revelation 19:10: "I am a fellow servant with you and with your brothers who hold to the testimony of Jesus. ...For the testimony of Jesus is the spirit of prophecy." The angel is instructing John to tell others of the mighty deeds (testimony) of Jesus—the Good News, the gospel—which is both mighty deeds and words.

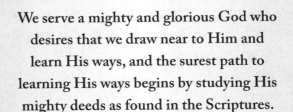

We serve a mighty and glorious God who desires that we draw near to Him and learn His ways, and the surest path to learning His ways begins by studying His mighty deeds as found in the Scriptures.

Perhaps we should allow the statement of Paul in Romans 15:17–19 to speak more clearly than the translators did, or those with Protestant cessationist glasses who domesticated Paul's words. There is an even stronger emphasis in the NIV to transform passages that are latent with implications of power into passages that are proclamations based on and dealing with the content of the message of reconciliation and forgiveness. Yet these passages in context are pregnant with implications regarding power—power to heal, power to deliver, power for miracles, as well as power for moral transformation.

The issue, then, is when we hear the word *gospel* today, do we tend to hear it through the voices of sixteenth-century reformers, whose focus was on salvation, rather than from the voices of the first-century missionaries, apostles, church planters, evangelists, healers, prophets, pastors, and teachers who saw the gospel more as *Christus Victor*—because of Jesus' death on the cross, His resurrection from the dead, and His ascension, He has won the victory over the strongman, the devil. As a result of this victory, in His name, not only is there forgiveness of sin and reconciliation to God resulting in eternal life, but there is also power over disease, demons, the devil, and damnation. Healing and miracles are part and parcel of the good news of the Kingdom. They are not primarily to confirm the message, but are to be an expression of the message, a part of the message.

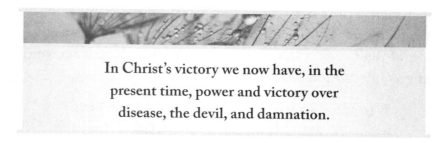

In Christ's victory we now have, in the
present time, power and victory over
disease, the devil, and damnation.

With the early Church there was a greater emphasis on Christus Victor—Jesus the Christ as Victor over sickness, disease, and demons with immediate benefits in this life for the believer. Over time this switched to Jesus, the one who saves us from hell and the author of eternal life. This moved the emphasis of the atonement from Christus Victor to substitutionary atonement. Both are true, but the former allows the proclaimer to offer whole life insurance instead of term life, which is the latter's message. The danger of the substitutionary atonement theory is that it places all or most of the benefit of the gospel in the next life. With the Christus Victor theory of the atonement, the cross has benefits not only in the next life but in this one as well, especially in regard to sickness, sin, and Satan. In Christ's victory, we now have in the present time, power and victory over disease, the devil, and damnation.

I do not want to be misunderstood—both of these understandings of the work of Jesus on the cross are important. Both are needed to complement the other, but when the substitutionary atonement understanding of the death of Jesus on the cross is seen as the only understanding, we lose part of the very heart of the gospel, and our ability to approach the throne of grace in our time of need with boldness is weakened.

In the Greek version of Romans 15: 19 the word *proclaimed* is missing. It has been added to the text during translation. In the following sentence I have given the meaning, in parentheses, of the Greek words, making it clear that there is no word in verse 19 for "proclaim" or "preach."

ἐν (in) δυνάμει (power) σημείων (signs) καὶ τεράτων (wonders), ἐν (in) δυνάμει (power) πνεύματος (spirit)· ὥστε (so that) με ἀπὸ (from) Ιερουσαλὴμ (Jerusalem) καὶ (and) κύκλῳ (circle) μέχρι (around) τοῦ Ιλλ υρικοῦ (Illyricum) πεπληρωκέναι (completely fulfilled) τὸ εὐαγγέλιον (good news of victory) τοῦ Χριστοῦ (of the Messiah) (Romans 15:19).

The Greek for "preach" or "preaching" (εὐαγγελίζω *euangelizō*) is the root of the same word found in verse 20, and translated as "proclaimed" or "preached." This word (εὐαγγελίζεσθαι *euaggelizesthai*) is not found in the Greek of verse 19. The word in verse 19 is *euangelion* (εὐαγγέλιον), which is the noun form of the word "gospel," not the verb form, which would be "to preach or proclaim the gospel."

Signs and wonders are to accompany the evangelical message—they belong together because the Word is powerful and effective to bring about reconciliation, forgiveness, new birth, and also healing and deliverance.

The proclamation of the rule of God—the age of grace—creates a healthy state in every respect. Bodily disorders are healed, and man's relationship to God is set right.[4] Joy reigns wherever the Word is proclaimed (see Acts 8:8). It brings salvation (σωτηρία—sōtāria; see 1 Cor. 15:1), it is deliverance, it is the way of salvation (ὑμῖν ὁδὸν σωτηρίας—humin hodon sōtārias; see Acts 16:17), and it effects regeneration (ἀναγεγεννημένοι—anagegennāmenoi; see 1 Pet. 1:23–25). It is not a word from man, but the living, eternal word of God.

The Holy Spirit, who was sought for the day of salvation, attests Himself now, in the time of fulfillment, when the glad tidings are proclaimed (see 1 Pet. 1:12). Hence, preaching is the powerful proclamation of the "good news" for salvation (σωτηρία—sōtāria) and carries with it authority and power. This would be missed if preaching the gospel (εὐαγγελίζεσθαι—euanggelizesthai) were to take place in human fashion or in wisdom speech (ἐν σοφίᾳ λόγου—en sophia logou; see 1 Cor. 1:17).

Paul is teaching a "full gospel," and this full gospel in context could not have been completely demonstrated or presented without the words and deeds—what was said and done—the signs and wonders, the healings and miracles. The word inaccurately translated "fully preached" means "to fulfill or fill up or complete." The text could be translated, " I have fulfilled the gospel," or "I have completed the gospel," or "I have filled up this region with the gospel."

Perhaps the best way to get the meaning in light of its context would be to say that Paul fully presented the gospel in what he *said* and what he *did*—by word and deed, by signs and wonders that accompanied the declaration of the good news and were part and parcel of the good news itself—that the Kingdom of God has broken upon the kingdom of the world, and Satan has been bound and his house is now being plundered.

Paul continues in Romans 15:20 "It has always been my ambition to preach the gospel where Christ was not known, so that I would not be building on someone else's foundation."

The NIV translation often goes amiss when it translates forms of *logos* or *rhema* as "message." Sometimes this is appropriate, but at other times it is too limiting. The word may be a prophecy or a word of knowledge, a word of command, or a declaration of faith, which is different than delivering a message or a sermon. Put another way, announcing what you are hearing from God is not the same as preaching a message. I believe the NIV emphasizes "message" to a fault, thereby limiting the broader meaning of the words *rhema* or *logos* and their derivatives.

## KNOW HIS WAYS, FIND HIS FAVOR

The promises of God are not a problem to be achieved, but a promise to be received.[5] When we learn to cooperate with the presence of God, ministry moves from laboring and striving to a place of rest. Moses understood how important it was to learn the ways of God directly from God in order to find favor with Him. A key Old Testament passage regarding this is found in Exodus:

> *The Lord would speak to Moses face to face, as a man speaks with his friend. Then Moses would return to the camp, but his young aide Joshua son of Nun did not leave the tent. Moses said to the Lord, "You have been telling me, 'Lead these people,' but you have not let me know whom you will send with me. You have said, 'I know you by name and you have found favor with me.' If you are pleased with me, teach me your ways so I may know you and continue to find favor with you. Remember that this nation is your people." The Lord replied, "My Presence will go with you, and I will give you rest." Then Moses said to him, "If your Presence does not go with us, do not send us up from here. How will anyone know that you are pleased with me and with your people unless you go with us? What else will distinguish me and your people from all the other people on the face of the earth?" And the Lord said to Moses, "I will do the very thing you have asked, because I am pleased with you and I know you by name." Then Moses said, "Now show me your glory"* (Exodus 33:11–18).

There are several things to be learned from this dialogue between Moses and God. First, learning the ways of God is dependent upon the presence of God and cannot be achieved by reducing our relationship with him to principles or precepts. God's mighty presence cannot be confined in a principle.

> When we learn to cooperate with the presence of God, ministry moves from laboring and striving to a place of rest.

Second, Moses understood the correlation between learning the ways of God and finding favor with Him. If we as believers are to co-labor with God to advance His Kingdom here on earth, we must know His ways. It is in that intimate relationship of knowing who God is that we find His enabling favor.

Third, Moses not only wanted to know God intimately; he also desired to see God's glory, for it is in His glory that His very presence abides.

Fourth, though not found specifically in this passage but in a larger study of Scripture, we learn that the primary way God reveals His glory in the Bible is through signs and wonders, healings and miracles.[6]

Unless we learn the ways of God, it is difficult to co-labor with Him. Without this knowledge we can miss His leadings and fail to experience the same level of faith that comes from knowing His will in a particular situation. When we know His ways and His will, we have greater faith that God will respond to our prayers of command, because we know that what we are commanding is in accordance with His will. The apostle John said it this way: "This is the confidence we have in approaching

God: that if we ask anything according to his will, he hears us. And if we know that he hears us—whatever we ask—we know that we have what we asked of him" (1 John 5:14).

# PART FOUR

# A HISTORY OF HEALING THEOLOGY AND SUPERNATURAL DEMONSTRATION

# CHAPTER 9

# EARLY CHURCH HISTORY AND DIVINE HEALING

Divine healing, a river which has flowed throughout the 2000-year history of the Church, was reduced to a small stream within historical Protestantism for about 500 years, but it never dried up completely. In the last hundred years it has become a raging river, stronger and more powerful than in any other century of the Church.

Church fathers and doctors of the Church give strong witness to this mighty river of divine healing. As we review historical accounts and consider the evidence, you will begin to understand why the Church lost its expectancy for the supernatural and its experience with divine healing, and how all of this is being restored.

The main impediment to the flow of God's healing in the Church comes from cessationist doctrine. *Cessationism* is the belief that all the healings and miracles in the Bible are historical. Cessationists believe that God did perform miracles and healings through His Son (Jesus) and through the early disciples, but He did so in order to establish correct doctrine through the writings of the apostles, which eventually became the Bible. Once His correct doctrine was established, healings and miracles, tongues, interpretation of tongues, and prophecies were no longer needed and so they ceased. For some the gift of prophecy was reinterpreted as preaching.

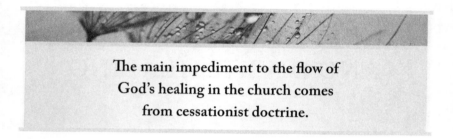

The main impediment to the flow of
God's healing in the church comes
from cessationist doctrine.

Furthermore, cessationism says that if miracles and healings are still possible, then the canon of the Bible would not be closed—there could be more Scriptures. But because the canon is closed and miracles and healings were to authenticate the message and the messengers, then gifts of healing are no longer in existence. If this is true, then God rarely intervenes in response to intercessory prayer; interventions are not to be expected as normative but as rare exceptions to the norm. For the last 500 years liberal and cessationist Protestant pastors have taught North American and European Churches not to believe or expect the gifts of healing and working of miracles to exist in the church. They have preached a powerless gospel outside of justification. This has caused many in the twentieth and twenty-first century to look to energy healing modalities such as Reiki, Therapeutic Touch and Healing Touch, which are not Christian in their worldview.[1]

Wesley and Count Zinzendorf, and many others who followed in their shoes, preached a gospel of justification *and* sanctification, with power for great moral transformation and liberation from sinful bondages. The Faith Cure movement, the Pentecostal movement, the Charismatic movement, and the Third Wave movement have all attempted to recover the gospel of Paul that needs to be fully proclaimed with not only justification and sanctification but also healing and deliverance.

The difficulty for cessationists is that their doctrine is not substantiated by the facts of history. An examination of the history of the Church and the biblical and theological foundations of healing repudiates cessationism. The "manifestation" and "power" gifts did not die out with the last of the original apostles, and Scripture bears witness to this truth. These "gifts" were given to the Church at Pentecost and have remained available to all believers throughout the history of the Church, and many have appropriated them to the glory of God.

## THE EARLY CHURCH FATHERS AND HEALING MIRACLES

The following excerpts are taken from the writings of the Ante-Nicene fathers, those who wrote before the Council of Nicea in A.D. 325. Their ministries of healing and deliverance give witness and testimony to the fact of the Spirit's miraculous gifts working in their time. These gifts of God's manifest power are core elements of the gospel of salvation to the whole man, not "emotional esoteric experiences" as some would try and characterize the signs and wonders in the history of the church down to the present day. Critics of Jonathan Edwards accused him of being involved with "strange fire" during the First Great Awakening. However, history sided with Edwards rather than his critic, Charles Chauncey.[2]

The Anti-Nicene fathers preached a Jesus who cared about releasing captives from demonic influences as well as freeing people from their bondage to sin. In short, they preached the Good News. They preached a Jesus of compassion who cared about the sickness of people's bodies as well as their souls. An emphasis upon the soul without concern for the body is indicative of Gnostic influence.[3]

**Justin Martyr** (A.D. 100–165) was an early church father who died a martyr's death. In his writings about the *charismata*, the gifts that God pours out upon believers, Martyr called attention to the power to heal as one of the particular gifts being received and used in his time.

In his "apology" addressed to the Roman Emperor he wrote, "For numberless demoniacs throughout the whole world, and in your city, many of our Christian men exorcizing them in the Name of Jesus Christ...have healed and do heal, rendering helpless and driving the possessing devils out of the men, though they could not be cured by all the other exorcists, and those who used incantations and drugs."[4]

**Tertullian** (A.D. 160–225) wrote a telling protest to the proconsul in North Africa during the persecutions there:

> The clerk of one of them [Roman officials], who was liable to be thrown upon the ground by an evil spirit, was set free from his affliction; as was also the relative of another, and the little boy of a third. And how many men of rank (to say nothing of common people) have been delivered from devils, and healed of diseases! Even Severus himself, the father of Antonine [the emperor], was graciously mindful of the Christians; for he sought out the Christian Proculus, surnamed Torpacion, the steward of Euhodias, and in gratitude for his having once

cured him by anointing, he kept him in his palace till the day of his death."[5]

Tertullian also explicitly identified persons who had been healed and testified to their great number and the wide range of physical and mental diseases represented.[6] Elsewhere, he said that God could, and sometimes did, recall men's souls to their bodies (raised them from the dead). He also believed in the continuation of the gifts from impartation at baptism. He wrote, "Therefore, you blessed ones, for whom the grace of God is waiting, when you come up from the most sacred bath of the new birth, when you spread out your hands for the first time in your mother's house with your brethren, ask your Father, ask your Lord, for the special gift of his inheritance, the distributed charisms.... Ask, he says, and you shall receive."[7]

**Origen** (A.D. 185–254) wrote his great treatise *Against Celsus,* which was aimed at the rulers of the pagan community of his time, with the express purpose of taking pagan thinking apart piece by piece. He makes note of how Christians "expel evil spirits, and perform many cures"—many of which he had himself witnessed, going on to say, "the name of Jesus can still remove distractions from the minds of men, and expel demons, and also take away diseases." In one of his letters, Origen tells of how baptism itself was sometimes the means by which a serious illness was cured, and that there were Christians who regained their health as a result and gave their lives to the Church because of such an experience.[8]

Perhaps the most interesting discussion of healing among the ante-Nicene fathers came from **Irenaeus** (A.D. 175–195) in Gaul, which is modern-day France. Irenaeus undoubtedly wrote more freely as he was somewhat removed from the danger of persecution centered in Rome that faced most of the early church fathers.

In *Against Heresies,* Irenaeus makes a strong statement that Christians can perform miracles and healings, which heretics are unable to do,[9] because heretics do not have access to the power of God and thus do not have the authority to heal. Unfortunately, these comments later became the basis for the skewed doctrine commonly taught today that says unless one's doctrine is 100 percent correct, any miracles or manifestations of the Spirit cannot be of God but are demonic in origin. This teaching ignores the fact that God is much more interested in whether or not we are relationally right with Him than in whether or not we have all our doctrinal ducks in a row (i.e. have right doctrine).

It is important to note that the first disciples in the early Church were sent out to heal the sick and set the demonized free long before they understood what we consider to be the most basic foundations of the Christian faith. I see this same dynamic in operation in the Church today. In Mozambique I have met Christian leaders who know little of the Bible and have very little theological training, but who are raising the dead in Jesus' name.

In a recent private meeting with an American apostolic leader from Cambodia, I was told that the top leaders in the Church in Cambodia do not believe it is important to teach a lot of biblical history in the early stages of discipleship. They have found it is much more important for disciples to be trained to flow in the gifts of the Spirit for power evangelism. He went on to say that a recent study had indicated that his work in Cambodia is where the Church is growing the fastest statistically. He also said that almost every church did not start as a result of their humanitarian work among the orphans and widows or the medical clinics or the water well drilling projects, but because healings and miracles were occurring in the area.[10]

Irenaeus attested to almost the same range of healings we find in the gospels and the book of Acts—all kinds of bodily infirmities as well as many different diseases were cured. He witnessed people healed of injuries from accidents and all manner of demons exorcised. He even described the raising of the dead. His pagan readers were well aware of these miracles of healing, as he makes clear, because this was often their path to conversion. To Irenaeus, no disease was impossible for God to heal. In fact, he believed that healing was a natural activity of Christians, performed to demonstrate the power of God.[11] He even spoke of prayer and fasting as an effective way to raise a person from the dead.[12]

It is of note that Irenaeus was writing primarily to refute the gnostic heresies of his day. The "secret knowledge" of Gnosticism taught a distinct separation of matter and spirit—that matter is evil and spirit is good. Therefore, what happens in the realm of the flesh, whether it be sickness or immorality, is of no importance. Because gnostic teaching devalued the natural body, assuming God was not interested in the welfare of the body, there was no value placed on the ministry of healing, and as a result there was no emphasis on healing. Many famous healers of the Pentecostal/Charismatic tradition in this century have been accused of being influenced by Gnosticism—of having a special understanding or revelation beyond Scripture or esoteric insight into "hidden" knowledge. How ironic that those accused of gnostic influence today are actually ministering in direct contradiction to basic gnostic assumptions! The ministry of Christ's compassion had no place in Gnosticism.

Further historical testimony to the Spirit's ongoing gifts can be found in the writings of Theophilus of Antioch (died c. 181), Arnobius and Lactantius from near the end of the Ante-Nicene period (300–325), and Quadratus, one of the earliest apologists, who wrote in Rome that the works of the Savior had continued to his time, and that the continued presence of men who had been healed left no question as to the reality of physical healing.[13]

## MIRACLES AND HEALINGS AMONG THE DOCTORS OF THE CHURCH

**Athanasius** (A.D. 296–393), along with four other Eastern theologians, wrote on healings that were occurring during his lifetime. These men were spiritual leaders of the Church, and they created the orthodoxy of the early Christian doctrines, which have changed little over time.[14]

**Gregory of Nazianzus** (A.D. 329–396) is said to have understood the roots of disease and how the Church is related to the job of the medical practitioner. He experienced two healings in his family, one when his sister was healed of a disease which caused fever and comatose-like experiences. Gregory's brother was also healed through prayer, and Gregory's mother was healed through a spiritual experience in a dream.[15]

**Basil the Great** (A.D. 329–379) was known for founding a Christian hospital. He saw no conflict between faith and healing, and viewed medical science as a last resort rather than a first choice in healing the sick.[16]

**Gregory of Nyssa** (A.D. 331–396) described healing as the main door through which knowledge of God reaches man. He recorded in great detail many healings, including those of a lame Roman soldiers and a once-blind child.[17]

**St. Augustine** (A.D. 354–430) was arguably the most prominent theologian in the West for 1,000 years. His influence is particularly important to the history of healing. In his early years of ministry, he wrote critically of healing and the miraculous. "These miracles are not allowed to continue into our time, lest the soul should always require things that can always be seen, and by becoming accustomed to them mankind should grow cold toward the very thing whose novelty had made men glow with fire."[18]

About forty years later he corrected this view. In his last and greatest work, *The City of God*, completed in 426, he includes a section that gives high value to the ongoing ministry of healing, noting that over seventy healings were recorded in his own bishopric of Hippo Regius in two years' time. After the healing of a blind man in Milan, Augustine wrote, "and so many other things of this kind have happened, even in this present time, that it is not possible for us either to know of all of them or to count up all of those of which we have knowledge."[19]

Later, Augustine's writings would have a tremendous impact on reformers Martin Luther and John Calvin. Even before the Reformation, Augustine's strong views of predestination and God's sovereignty would change the view of the Church from the historic "Warfare Worldview" to a "Blueprint Worldview."[20]

Rather than looking at the consequences of sin's curse as the work of the enemy that the Church has the authority and power to come against—to continue the work of Christ who came "to destroy the devil's work" (1 John 3:8)—Christians began to see all things as foreordained and therefore to passively accept what they believed to be God's will. Ultimately, this shift from a warfare worldview to a blueprint worldview would have a distinctly negative impact upon the theology of healing in the Church. For the sake of historical accuracy, it's important to remember that before Augustine died, he became known for a healing anointing and the authority to deliver the demonized.[21]

> Before Augustine died, he became
> known for a healing anointing and the
> authority to deliver the demonized.

Augustine also believed in the continuation of the gifts into his day and had much to say about the baptism in the Holy Spirit and the charisms of the Spirit. In relationship to water baptism, he stated, "We must not think that those who have received a valid baptism have also automatically (*continuo*) received the Holy Spirit."[22] Augustine's quote, in context, is referring to the baptism in the Holy Spirit. When Christianity became the official religion of the empire, the standards for entry were lowered, and the degree of sincerity was lower for many of the so-called converts. With this change, the expectation for the charisms to be given, even manifested at baptism, became less and less.

# CHAPTER 10

# THE FIRST 400 YEARS OF CHURCH HISTORY: AN ERA OF HEALING AND MIRACLES

As we look back over the first 400 or more years of Church history, we hear the early fathers collectively saying, "Miracles have not stopped. They still occur today!" So why then do we have such division within the Church today on this issue? How did the Church, which witnessed so much healing its first thousand years, become so closed and skeptical about this vital ministry? I believe we have erred by focusing the redemption we have in Christ almost totally in the future, while making only moral changes available in this present life. This was not the understanding or the focus of the early Church.

The early community of Christians believed in a present power not only for moral change but also for authority over demons, power over sickness and disease, and the experience of the reality of spiritual gifts in their lives, especially in the corporate life of gathered congregations. Today, we have emptied the Atonement (the cross) of its full effect by an understanding that is correct as far as it goes—substitutionary atonement. Unfortunately, this understanding does not go far enough. It must be balanced by other understandings of the atoning work of Jesus on the cross, especially the *Christus Victor* understanding of atonement. It is only when we understand the fullness of what occurred on the cross that we can fully comprehend all that Jesus did for us in His scourging and crucifixion.

Does God still anoint people to move in signs and wonders? When we see ministries of miraculous healing, deliverance, even the raising of the dead, can we be sure this is truly of God? What about meetings where there is a tangible sense of the supernatural and we witness all manner of emotional and physical responses? Can this be the work of the Holy Spirit? Much of mainstream Christianity in Europe and North America today would answer, "No." But the majority of Christians in Asia, Africa, and Latin America would answer a resounding, "Yes!" This is why historical context is important to our understanding of how the Church has been influenced in her interpretation of Scripture.

The early community of Christians believed in a present power not only for moral change but also for authority over demons, power over sickness and disease, and the experience of the reality of spiritual gifts in their lives.

## THE MIRACLES AND HEALINGS OF MARTIN LUTHER

On October 30, 1517, **Martin Luther** nailed his 95 Theses to the door of the Wittenberg Church in Germany and the

Reformation "officially" began. Neither Luther nor Calvin ever challenged the Aquinas-Aristotelian[1] synthesis in their writing. Despite his philosophical bias, in 1540 Luther successfully prayed for his fellow reformer and systematizer of Lutheran doctrine Philip Melancthon to be healed as he lay near death. Instead of a "thy will be done" approach, Luther found a "my will be done" declaration. How interesting. It is sad that so few Lutherans are aware of this side of Luther's ministry. The following occurred July 2, 1540.

> Melancthon was on his way to the scene of these deliberations when, brooding over this unhappy affair, his fears and scruples brought on a sickness just as he had reached Weimar, which laid him nigh to death's door. Intelligence of his state was conveyed to Wittenberg, and Luther, in the Elector's carriage, hastened to Weimar. He found Philip, on his arrival, apparently all but dead; understanding, speech, and hearing had left him, his countenance was hollow and sunk, his eyes closed, and he seemed in a death-like sleep. Luther expressed his astonishment to the companions of his journey, "How shamefully has the devil handled this creature!" and then, according to his custom, turning to the window, he prayed with all his might. He reminded God of his promises from the Holy Scriptures, and implored him now to fulfill them, or he could never trust in them again. [Author's emphasis; also note how much this sounds like the prayer of a "Word of Faith" minister.] Rising from prayer he took Melancthon's hand, and called to him in a cheerful tone, "Take heart, Philip: you shall not die. God

has reason enough to kill you, but 'He willeth not the death of the sinner, but rather that he should repent and be saved.' He desires life, not death. The greatest sinners that ever lived on earth—Adam and Eve—were accepted of God in his grace; far less will he give you up, Philip, and let you perish in your sins and faintheartedness. Give no room to despondency: be not your own murderer; but throw yourself on your Lord, who killeth and maketh alive." At these words Melancthon evinced a sudden restoration, as though from death to life; he drew his breath with energy; and after a while turning his face to Luther, implored him "not to stay him; he was on a good journey; and nothing better could befall him." Luther replied, "Not so, Philip, you must serve our Lord God yet longer." And when Melancthon had gradually become more cheerful, Luther, with his own hands, brought him something to eat, and overruled his repugnance with the threat, "Hark, Philip, you shall eat, or I excommunicate you!"

Lutheran reformer and intimate friend of Martin Luther Friedrich Myconius (1490–1546) was sick and about to die, rapidly sinking in consumption. Myconius sent word to Luther that he "was sick, not for death, but for life." Luther commenced to pray fervently that Myconius "might not pass through the veil to rest, whilst he was left out-of-doors amid the devils," and wrote to his friend that he felt certain his prayers would be heard, and by God's mercy his days would be lengthened, so that he would survive Luther. Myconius was raised up again from the brink of the grave, and eventually outlived Luther by seven weeks.[2]

Luther's actual prayer ended with, "Farewell dear Frederick. The Lord grant that I may not hear of your departure while I am still living. May he cause you to survive me. This I pray. This I wish. *My will be done.* Amen. For it is not for my own pleasure but for the glory of God's name that I wish it."[3]

Sometime later Luther remarked about this time of prayer for Frederick and Philip. After snatching Philip from the arms of death, Luther described his bold prayer: "In this instance our Lord God had to pay me; for I threw the bag of concern before his door and I dinned his ears with all of his promises as to how he desired to favorably hear our prayer—promises which I well knew how to document in Scripture! I put it to him that he had to grant my request if he expected me to continue to trust his promises."[4]

While looking for the quote of Luther's prayer for Myconius, I discovered a very interesting book written in 1832 called *The Suppressed Evidence: Or Proofs of the Miraculous Faith and Experience of the Church of Jesus Christ in All Ages,* by the Reverend Thomas Boys, M.A., of Trinity College Cambridge. It too gives evidence that even the Reformers themselves believed in miracles and in the possibility of miracles occurring in their time.[5]

## WHY THE REFORMERS REJECTED THE MIRACULOUS

Both Calvin and Luther felt keenly compelled to challenge the authority of the Catholic Church. While what follows is greatly over-simplified, their reasoning went something like this: "Because the Catholics are using healings to validate their false traditions, the healings must either be false or the work of the devil." It is not hard to understand the animosity of the reformers and why they so vehemently threw out anything that might bolster what they considered a grossly illegitimate claim to spiritual authority. Simply remember the horrors of their day, all done in the name of God. Catholics and Protestants were being viciously persecuted, tortured, and burned at the stake by religious systems that had long lost touch with the word of God's emphasis upon *power and love*. The reformers cried out for a return to the objective authority of Scripture and, in the process, became quite anti-supernatural. An examination of the specifics of their rejection is revealing.

During this same time period of the reformation, a group called the Anabaptists appeared on the scene. These Anabaptists were having subjective, revelatory experiences of prophecy. Calvin and Luther felt that these experiences further threatened and undermined a return to the authority of Scripture, especially when those prophecies did not line up with the word. However, the rise of a skeptical age was not just caused by what was happening in the Church; it was also caused by what was happening in science.

## THE AGE OF REASON AND INTELLECTUALISM

The sixteenth and seventeenth centuries in Europe ushered in the scientific revolution and with it the Age of Reason, which sprang from the perceived need to reject the supernatural and profoundly affected the Church's interpretation of Scripture. Skepticism flourished toward anything that did not have a material, natural explanation that fell within the limits of human comprehension and logic, as well as conforming to Newtonian physics.

Both the scientific revolution and the Age of Reason coupled to radically change the landscape of theology regarding present-day supernatural works of God. "Higher criticism," which explained away all the miracles of the Bible in natural terms, first arose in German universities. Within fifty years, a rejection of the supernatural for today was taught in most U.S. seminaries. By the late 1800s, it was widely taught that even biblical "miracles" never happened. "Right reasoning" was on the throne, taking precedence over divine revelation and experience. If it could not be explained in naturalistic rather than super-naturalistic understanding, it did not happen.

## FUNDAMENTALISM

Fundamentalism entered the scene as a backlash to liberal theology but only addressed the issue of biblical inerrancy and inspiration. Neither liberals nor fundamentalists had a theology of the miraculous, particularly healing. Fundamentalists viewed the miracles of the Bible as something that was needed only for the apostolic age to confirm and establish a new message. Once the gospel had been kick-started and codified in Scripture, fundamentalists believed miracles were no longer necessary.

It is interesting that today, in regard to the gifts of the Holy Spirit, Pentecostals have more in common with Catholics than they do with other Protestants, because Catholics have never been cessationist in their doctrine. John Wimber once told me that those who have the hardest time receiving healing are certain Protestants, while those who receive the easiest are Catholics because Catholics are more open to the miraculous.[6]

However, the Holy Spirit was not going to leave historical Protestantism to itself and its doubts. He was determined to break in upon the historical Protestant movement and take His Church back.

## HEALING IN PROTESTANTISM

Healing ministry in historical Protestantism began in Europe before coming to the Americas. One of the earliest Protestants to have a healing ministry was George Fox, founder of the Society of Friends (Quakers). When he ministered in the colonies of North America in 1672 there were reports of many healings as he prayed with the laying on of hands. He wrote a book on miracles in which he recorded about 150 healings in his ministry.[7]

Another early group was the Brethren who were persecuted German Pietists who later settled in the Pennsylvania colony. They practiced the anointing with oil found in James 5:14-15. In time, this group split into four denominational groups, but all kept the emphasis on healing.[8] Eduard Irving and his National Scottish Church in London began seeing healings in 1830. Irving would impact John Alexander Dowie who considered Irving the most influential person in his life.[9] In 1842 a miraculous healing movement began in Germany with the highly educated Lutheran theologian/pastor Johann Blumhardt.[10] The Adventist movement led by Ellen White believed in healing in the late 1840s, but gradually this emphasis was replaced with dietary and healthful living.[11] Dorothea Trudel began having healings through her prayers in 1851 in Switzerland. She was a young florist. She ended up opening several faith homes where they prayed for the sick. Samuel Zeller was her assistant and successor. Otto Stockmeyer was introduced to healing through

Samuel Zeller in 1867 and several years later wrote his book on healing, *Sickness and the Gospel*.[12] A. J. Gordon would call him the "theologian of the doctrine of healing by faith."[13]

According to Dr. Paul Chappell, the American Holiness movement provided the most significant theological environment for healing by faith in America. The instantaneous sanctification through confessing until the possession of the experience, emphasized by Charles Finney and Phoebe Palmer in the 1830s, became the springboard to receive healing through the same method because both were in the atonement of Christ.[14] In 1846, Ethan Allen, considered the father of the healing movement in America, connected the doctrine of Christian perfection with healing. He had been healed by Methodists in 1846 and became the first American minister to make faith healing his full-time work.[15] There were many who would be instrumental in propagating the new message of healing in America. The following are some of the highlights and the most important people in the healing movements.

### Charles Cullis

According to Chappell, "Charles Cullis, a homoeopathic doctor in Boston, did more than any other person to propagate faith healing and to draw the attention of the American Church to the doctrine."[16] Cullis' personal story is amazing. After reading the *Life of Dorothea Trudel* he was convicted that healing was for today and was appropriated by the prayer of faith. Cullis exerted tremendous impact through his involvement with the Holiness leaders and with the beginnings of the Faith Cure Movement. He would experience his first healing in 1870, when a girl who was immobilized for five months from a brain tumor was healed. He would eventually lead many of the most important leaders of the holiness movement to accept the message of healing.

Cullis went to Europe in 1873 for four months, where he studied the ministries of Johann Blumhardt, Dorothea Trudel, and George Muller. (Muller did not have a faith healing home or room, but his whole ministry was underwritten by faith for the needs of thousands of orphans he cared for.) Cullis then began conducting internationally known camp meetings on holiness and healing. These faith conventions brought the subject of divine healing into the public eye.[17] The published work of Dr. Charles Cullis proved to be the most important instrument in catapulting the issue of healing forward and would become the most important theological question in the nineteenth century.

### The Wonder Stage of the Divine Healing Movement

R. Kelso Carter called the period from 1881–1885 the "wonder" stage of the divine healing movement, with many healing conventions held during this period. Carter's book, *The Atonement of Sin and Sickness; or a Full Salvation for Soul and Body*, published in 1884, was seen as the most powerful defense of all the books on healing. Carter also wrote the famous song, "Standing on the Promises of God."

Other important nineteenth-century books on healing include *The Lord that Healeth Thee*, published in 1881 by William Boardman, a leader of the Keswick Holiness movement; *The Ministry of Healing: Miracles of Cure in All Ages*, published in 1882 by A. J. Gordon, a famous Baptist pastor/scholar; *Gospel Parallelisms: Illustrated in the Healing of the Body and Soul*, published in 1883 by R. L. Stanton, former president of Miami University in Ohio and a moderator of the general assembly of the Presbyterian Church; and *Faith Healing: A Defense, or The Lord Thy Healer,* published in 1889 by R. L. Marsh.[18]

Many of the famous evangelical leaders of this time period were involved in praying for the sick—something that I never heard of in my religious studies major at university and during my seminary training. For example, "a significant healing ministry was conducted at Metropolitan Tabernacle, pastored by Charles H. Spurgeon, one of the most famous Baptist preachers in Baptist history. Most of Spurgeon's healing ministry took place through his pastoral visitation, although he also spoke on the topic and regularly prayed for the sick from his pulpit. Spurgeon's biographer reports that it was common for parishioners to request the prayers of the church for healing and that thousands of cases of healings could be documented."[19]

Other famous Christian leaders in the healing movement include men like Andrew Murray, a Dutch Reformed pastor who was healed and then taught on healing;[20] and Eduard Irving, the Presbyterian pastor of a prestigious church in London and the founder of the Apostolic Catholic Church. Irving was among the first Protestants to teach a restoration of all the gifts of the Spirit to the Church today. His teachings were so threatening to cessationism that B.B. Warfield spent a whole chapter in his book *Counterfeit Miracles* disputing Irving. Most of Warfield's comments were *ad hominem* (against the man), and little of the chapter actually dealt with Irving's arguments.

A.B. Simpson, the Presbyterian pastor who founded the Christian and Missionary Alliance denomination, was used of God to rebirth faith for healing among Protestants.[21] Alexander Dowie, a Holiness preacher, is considered by some to be the most important of the healers of this time period; however, he would not end well.[22] After the death of his daughter he became eccentric, believed himself to be the prophet Elijah, and made several decisions that were embarrassing to the Church.[23] Both John G. Lake and F.F. Bosworth would come out of Dowie's church to begin their own healing ministries.

Charles S. Price, a Methodist with a law degree from Oxford,[24] and Aimee Semple McPherson were the most important healers of the 1920s and 1930s, along with F.F. Bosworth, whose book *Christ the Healer*[25] is still a classic today. Price's book *The Real Faith* has a great perspective and understanding on the kind of faith and the source of such faith for healings and miracles to occur; however, instead of translating the text as "have faith *in* God" it should be translated "have the faith *of* God."[26]

### Emergence of Spirit-Empowered Christianity

With the arrival of Pentecostals on the scene, John G. Lake, one of the earliest Pentecostal healing evangelists, emerged. His sermons contain important insights to early Pentecostal beliefs.[27] Lake had a tremendous healing gift and also trained others for healing. He believed a great healing revival was imminent, but he would die in 1947, one year shy of the revival that peaked during the years from 1948 to 1958, a revival noted for healing and the gifts of the Spirit.

This peak season of revival was birthed through the ministry of William Branham, whose influence extended to both the Latter Rain Revival that began in 1947 and the 1948 Healing Revival. Some of the key leaders in the 1948 Healing Revival included William Branham, Oral Roberts, Jack Coe, T.L. Osborne, and A.A. Allen.[28]

The 1948 healing revival was followed by the Charismatic movement, which began in the early 1960s. Kathryn's

Kuhlman's ministry, which began in 1946,[29] would draw heavily from those who were becoming part of the Charismatic movement, which was made up of several streams. One stream consisted of those who did not leave their denominations to join Pentecostal denominations. This stream believed all the gifts of the Holy Spirit still exist today and that their operation should be normative rather than rare or seldom. Many Catholics and Anglicans would become part of the Charismatic movement. Among the most famous of the Catholics would be Father Francis MacNutt and Father John Bertolucci.

### *Word of Faith Movement*

Another stream that emerged within the Charismatic movement was the Word of Faith stream. The most famous preachers to emerge from the Word of Faith stream would be Kenneth Hagin, Kenneth Copeland, and Charles Capps.[30] This group has been severely criticized, even by *The Dictionary of Pentecostal and Charismatic Movements* by Burgess. In referring to Hagin's ministry, Paul Chappell, who wrote the article on "Healing Movements," stated, "Hagin's theology is a unique blend of evangelical orthodoxy, biblical fundamentalism, Charismatic theology, and metaphysical thought. He differs from most advocates of divine healing in his use of positive confession, sensory denial (particularly as it relates to physical symptoms of illness), and implicit rejection of medical science. Criticism of these latter aspects of his teachings on healing has come from within the Charismatic movement because of their origin in the metaphysical teachings of New Thought/Christian Science as presented by E.W. Kenyon. Hagin has been significantly influenced by Kenyon in these areas."[31] Chappell attributed some of Kenyon's insights to metaphysical or New Thought, but that has been refuted by the writings of Paul

King and Joe McIntyre, and I agree with the conclusions of King and McIntyre rather than Chappell.[32]

I believe Dr. Paul Chappell is wrong and was influenced by one or all of the following: the writings of Dave Hunt in *Seduction of Christianity*[33] and *Beyond Seduction;*[34] Dan R. McConnell in *A Different Gospel;*[35] John MacArthur in *Charismatic Chaos;*[36] and Hank Hanegraaff in *Christianity in Crisis;*[37] especially *A Different Gospel* by McConnell.

Dr. Paul King, a professor at Oral Roberts University and a Christian and Missionary Alliance minister, has written a much more balanced explanation of the issues. Drawing upon Joe McIntyre's *E.W. Kenyon and His Message of Faith: The True Story,* King evaluates both the modern Word of Faith movement and the Faith Cure movement in light of the accusations raised by McConnell and Hanegraaff. In his book, *Only Believe: Examining the Origin and Development of Classic and Contemporary Word of Faith Theologies,* King argues that connecting Word of Faith to New Thought metaphysics is historically inaccurate.[38] It is of note that Pastor McIntyre had the good fortune of receiving Kenyon's personal diary, which contained the dates of his life. Based upon this diary, it became obvious that the charges of a metaphysical influence on his teaching were definitely and beyond question proven to be unfounded. Instead, it was found that the true influence upon Kenyon was the holiness movement and the writing of the Baptist A. J. Gordon, whom he quotes more than any other source.[39]

### The Future of Spirit-Empowered Christianity and Divine Healing

In the last quarter of the twentieth century healing evangelists like Reinhard Bonnke and Benny Hinn became known in the Americas. At the same time, Omar Cabrera and Carlos Annacondia became known through their healing ministries in Argentina as well as others with powerful ministries, whom I do not know well but know of, who are in Africa and Asia.

In the first decade of the twenty-first century, God has been at work around the globe, raising up an army of healers—men like Henry Madava and Sunday Adalaja of Kiev, Ukraine, both of whom have powerful healing ministries; Claudio Freidzon in Argentina; Leif Hetland in Pakistan; and many in Africa. Coming out of North America and impacting nations worldwide, God has raised up the leaders of the Revival Alliance, which include Bill Johnson, Rolland and Heidi Baker, John Arnott, Che Ahn, Georgian Banov, and myself, Randy Clark.

Heidi Baker's greatest gift for healing occurs in Mozambique, Che Ahn's in Asia, Bill Johnson's in Australia, Georgian Banov's in Europe, John Arnott's in England, and mine in Russia, Ukraine, and Brazil, especially Brazil. Beginning in 2011 I have witnessed a great increase in healing in Asia in my meetings. Additionally, all of the members of the Revival Alliance are now seeing an increase in the number of powerful healings in the United States.

## HEALING AS AN EXPRESSION OF THE GOSPEL

There is a difference between confirming the gospel and confirming doctrines and Scripture. A study of the New Testament indicates that the function or purpose of healings and miracles is to be part of the expression of the gospel. The gifts, including healings and miracles, are part of the "good news" of the in-break of the Kingdom of God and are to continue until

Jesus' second coming. They are the energies of God that make the power and presence of God tangible today, the means by which the "strong man's house is plundered" (see Matt. 12:29; Mark 3:27). They display the mercy and love of God as found in Jesus and should never have been separated from His gospel.

# PART FIVE

# HOW WE LOST OUR INHERITANCE

# CHAPTER 11

# THE CHURCH MOVES AWAY FROM HEALING

Spiritual gifts flourished in the first-century Church and continued until institutionalism and a shift from theistic to deistic Christianity brought about the demise of the charismata. As a result of this shift we (the Church) abdicated the power (and authority) to push back the dominion of the god of this world, the devil. As we have noted, "The two most representative forms of the practical deistic version of Christianity are liberalism and cessationism. I am sure neither group would consider themselves as deists, but for practical purposes, their theology regarding the supernatural activity of God in the world through his gifts or energies ends up with a practical deistic outlook."[1] This evolution of Christian theology away from the New Testament emphasis on healing, exorcism, and miracles led to the practice of going so far as to deny their contemporary occurrence.

This unbelief in the miraculous has played itself out historically in various ways within both Protestantism and Catholicism. Some of the material that I am going to cover in these next two chapters can be found in some of my other books. I am including it here because I feel it is very pertinent to our study of our authority to heal and thus worthy of review for those who are familiar with it and for serious consideration and study for those who are not. We must have at least a basic understanding of the various movements and factors within the Church that have impacted the ministry of healing if we are to gain a clear picture of the current state of healing in the Church today.

## THE DEMISE OF THE CHARISMATA

As the fledgling Church of Jesus Christ spread throughout the known world and gained in size and strength, institutionalism crept in, beginning with Ignatius, Bishop of Caesarea (A.D. c. 35–c. 110). The writings of Ignatius, which focused on a number of theological issues pertinent to the early Church including the role of bishop, gave the Church some of its earliest theology. Appointed to the position of bishop, Ignatius is considered among the earliest apostolic fathers of the Church and the one who most prominently delineated local church hierarchy. Some historians believe he knew the apostle John, which may have contributed to the eventual practice of apostolic succession as a means of protecting the Church from heretical teachers. As structure increased with the introduction of ecclesiastical offices beginning with Ignatius, spontaneous manifestations of the power of God grew less desirable to those in authority, culminating in a shift in spiritual authority away from the one possessing the spiritual gift to the one occupying the ecclesiastical office. The spiritual authority of the laity given by the Holy Spirit eroded to such an extent that it essentially ceased, replaced by ceremonial ritual and clerical order.

On the heels of this shift came the Edict of Milan in A.D. 315, making Christianity the legal religion of the Roman

Empire.[2] The persecution that had kept the early Church largely pure gave way to a flood of nominal believers seeking power and influence rather than God. This led those in authority in the Church to hold ever more tightly to the reins. Eventually, Church and state merged, increasing the structure and formality of the way in which the Church functioned. The New Testament model of Church in which the gifts flowed in the midst of worship was replaced by highly stylized ritual presided over by clergy. In the midst of this paradigm shift were those who held fast to the spiritual gifts and were often marginalized and labeled as heretics.

> Whereas sickness had once been viewed as something to be healed of, it was now seen as a blessing. This caused the ministry of healing to diminish greatly as many now considered it unnecessary.

Because of the close ties between Church and state, between the fall of the Roman Empire in A.D. 476 and the beginnings of the Protestant Reformation in the early sixteenth century and the periods of societal chaos that occurred, the Church underwent a period of significant theological change. Medieval monasticism yielded many devout believers and more than a few unfortunate colorful characters whose exaggerated spiritual antics caused the Church to draw further away from the miraculous. A form of monasticism, called mysticism, developed and was often characterized by extreme asceticism, which often took the form of prolonged physical suffering. This extreme asceticism combined with Greek thought that valued the spirit but despised the body led to the theology that said through suffering we can better identify with Christ. Whereas sickness had once been viewed as something to be healed of, it was now seen as a blessing. This caused the ministry of healing to diminish greatly as many now considered it unnecessary.

## THE AGE OF REASON AND INTELLECTUALISM

As we noted in Chapter 10, the scientific revolution of the sixteenth and seventeenth centuries, accompanied by the Age of Reason, led to the advent of "higher criticism" that began in German universities and spread to U.S. seminaries, dealing a blow to the belief in the supernatural and eventually resulting in outright rejection of the supernatural in the life and work of the Church today.

Rene Descartes (1596–1650) and Baruch Spinoza (1632–1677) were among the many philosophers of that era who gave us what is termed modern rationalism. Drawing on the works of ancient philosophers such as Pythagoras, Plato, and Aristotle, these rationalists proposed that reason is the chief source and test of knowledge, not experience. Rationalism says that truth can only be attained through our intelligence and the use of deductive reasoning. Scientific rationalism's departure from Judeo-Christian thinking led many in the Church to deny miracles and healings.

Humanism, with roots in Renaissance humanism (fourteenth to sixteenth centuries), dealt yet another blow to the miraculous. Taking a rational, non-religious approach to life, humanism puts forth the idea that human virtue can be created by our human reason alone, independent from our traditional (Christian) religious beliefs. Humanism has a long history beginning in the Renaissance in reaction to religious authoritarianism in medieval Catholicism. The Age of Enlightenment brought another round of humanism in reaction to dogmatic Protestantism, leading to a more secular orientation that manifested itself in philosophies such as existentialism, Marxism, atheism, and what we now call secular humanism. Secular humanism has replaced religion for many in today's modern world.

The advance of medical science brought the loss of the belief in the human soul,[3] causing a rejection of the traditional view and reducing humans to an expression of chemical impulses interacting with each other. The result was that the humanist movement dehumanized humankind. Because the unity of body, soul, and spirit was denied, modern allopathic medicine began treating patients' symptoms with surgery or pharmaceuticals rather than treating the underlying causes of sickness.[4]

The end result of all of these things for the Church is that today we still have many Christians who reject the miraculous. We have what I call *unbelieving believers*—those who have committed themselves to be followers of Jesus Christ and been regenerated by the Holy Spirit but do not believe that certain gifts of the Holy Spirit are for the Church today—and *believing unbelievers*—those who have not been regenerated by the Holy Spirit and have not committed their lives to following Jesus Christ but are completely open to the power of God and the gifts of healing in operation today and who experience healings outside the walls of the church. Lately, I have been thinking that there should be a third type of believer in addition to the *unbelieving believers* and the *believing unbelievers*. The third category would be the *believing confused believers*. This latter category is made up of those who believe in the supernatural, but who are confused about their relationship to Christ. They might belong to a denomination and even attend church, but they are so deceived in their understanding of their relationship to the supernatural and to Jesus Christ that though they believe in the supernatural power to heal, they may be either nominally saved, have had a false conversion, or at best are confused carnal believers in their relationship to Jesus.

## THE STORY OF A BELIEVING CONFUSED BELIEVER

A powerful example of a believing confused believer is the story of Martha Wertz, a shaman healer who was introduced to the supernatural healing realm through her Methodist church and who believed it was possible to be a Methodist Christian and a practicing shaman at the same time. What follows is a synopsis of her story from her forthcoming book.[5]

Martha grew up in a home that was emotionally and spiritually chaotic, setting the stage for a New Age lifestyle that captivated her for more than three decades and nearly destroyed her life, her children, and her marriage. In her teens, her father's job necessitated relocation to South America. There in the city of Rio de Janeiro, Martha and her family were bombarded daily by the Macumba witchcraft of the region. The nominal Christian background of her childhood left Martha and her family unprepared for the spiritually demonic onslaught that assailed them during their time in South America and beyond. Instead of strenuously avoiding the occult practices that were all around them, they began to unknowingly embrace certain elements of the demonic under the guise of cultural awareness. This seemingly innocent exposure and participation opened a door to the demonic that was not closed until many years later.

Back in the U.S., as a young woman just out of college Martha developed an interest in holistic and natural healing methods, born largely out of a frustration with allopathic medicine's failure to provide healing for her and her family over the years. With no biblical discernment to draw upon, she began to consult various New Age practitioners for a variety of ailments and quickly became "hooked" by the sense of belonging she found in the New Age community. Over the ensuing fifteen years she became a Reiki[6] master of renown, speaking at professional conferences. Well-meaning and sincere, Martha sought to help others, although she never witnessed any actual healing from Reiki or any of the other occult-based practices she used.

During these years Martha's interest in New Age practices continued to grow. She studied another energy healing modality called Healing Touch, consulted psychics, sought communication with angels and the dead, and eventually became a full-fledged shaman healer. Shamans are medicine men and women who are trained to communicate with the spirit world, relying heavily on occult spiritual practices that include animism. Shamanic work promises freedom and long-term healing and delivers neither, while opening the door to sorcery, white and black magic, and demonic principalities and powers.

In the midst of all of this, Martha's marriage began to crumble and she and her children came under increasing attack. Her eldest son was plagued by violent fits during which he would shout obscenities and claw at himself while writhing on the floor. Shadowy figures appeared to Martha and the children repeatedly during the night, and during the day, would turn into snarling creatures when confronted. Desperate, Martha turned to the occult community for help, unaware she was actually fueling the demonic fires in her home. It was at this point that God intervened.

While channel surfing one day, Martha happened upon a TV show featuring a popular female evangelist. What she heard peaked her interest and she kept tuning in daily. Gradually, the truth of God's word began to pierce the darkness that had overtaken her mind. About this same time, her mother was diagnosed with terminal cancer. Martha packed up their children and went to live with her mother in order to help her through the remaining months of her life. Martha's husband stayed behind in another part of the country for the next nine months. Little did she know that this move was a "rescue mission" of sorts. God pulled her and her children out of a home and a lifestyle under siege by the devil and brought them into a place where Christian community would help them find deliverance from the occult and the healing and freedom in Christ they so desperately needed.

Over the course of the next nine months the Holy Spirit lovingly revealed Himself to Martha countless times, gently teaching the truth of God's word to her. Slowly she and the children began to purge their lives of the occult. At one point they got Martha's mother to agree to let them get rid of her collection of "cultural" (occult) masks from around the world. Together with her sister, they tried to burn some of the scariest ones, but despite being made of wood the masks would not burn until they had prayed over them and anointed them with oil.

Purging these masks marked the beginning of God's instructions to start cleaning out all objects in her life that had been inspired by Satan, and it was a turning point spiritually for Martha and her family. She began to attend a Spirit-filled church where she experienced the presence of God and the power of the gospel. Her children joined youth groups and her husband met up with a powerful prayer team in the form of a Christian men's group that was able to support and sustain him through the trails of having his family living far away. Eventually, through sound biblical teaching and supportive Christian community, Martha came to understand that the occult practices she had embraced were an abomination to God (see Deut. 18:9–13).

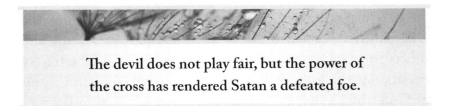

The devil does not play fair, but the power of
the cross has rendered Satan a defeated foe.

With her eyes opened in a whole new way she began a deeper purge of her home and her life. Over a period of several months she filled a large dumpster with New Age materials worth thousands of dollars. Realizing that cleansing was needed in the spiritual as well as the natural, she began Sozo counseling sessions. During these sessions, Jesus peeled back layer after layer, setting her free in the authority of His name.

The final phase of Martha's deliverance came as a result of attending one of Global Awakening's conferences on the topic of New Age versus Christian healing. It was there that she came face to face with the realization that she had aligned her identity with the Kingdom of Satan. Bitter and angry that she had been conned and horrified that she had dragged her family and friends into the occult, Martha was finally able to shed the last vestiges of the deception that had exercised a stranglehold on her life for far too long. A New Age journey that had been decades in the making and had consumed years of her and her family's life finally came to an end.

Martha will be the first to tell you that it takes time to heal the past and to allow God to build a new foundation. Most people will go through periods of recovery, re-creation, and reorganization on many levels as they learn how to recognize and keep the enemy out of their life. The devil does not play fair, but the power of the cross has rendered Satan a defeated foe.

It is of importance to note from Martha's story how the Church utterly failed to teach, train, and protect Martha and others from the wiles of the enemy. This is part of the trap of cessationist thinking. When you deny the presence and power of God, you are left with no resources with which to fight an enemy that you don't acknowledge exists.

# CHAPTER 12

# CHURCH FACTORS AND THE DECLINE OF HEALING

## UNBELIEF PLAYS OUT IN PROTESTANTISM

As I noted earlier, the two most representative forms of the practical deistic version of Christianity are liberalism and cessationism. Both of these deistic versions—along with neo-orthodoxy, dispensationalism, fundamentalism, and new liberalism—have had a very negative impact on the Church's faith in healings and miracles. In my experience, up until quite recently one was hard-pressed to find a seminary that did not teach skepticism regarding the miraculous today, outside the Pentecostal and Charismatic schools. One exception that I know of is United Theological Seminary (UTS) in Dayton, Ohio. UTS is a Methodist seminary that was at one time quite liberal but now seeks to position itself as a place noted for faith and committed to renewal of the Holy Spirit. This change at UTS came about to a considerable degree due to the influence of the Randy Clark Scholars program that is currently part of the doctoral degree program at UTS.

## LIBERALISM

Theological or Protestant liberalism sprang from the German Enlightenment (nineteenth century), most particularly from philosophers Friedrich Schleiermacher and Immanuel Kant, who approached anything that had been previously accepted as true with skepticism. With its emphasis on experience over scriptural authority and ethics over doctrine, liberalism (liberal theology) embraces higher biblical criticism,[1] which has its roots in rationalism and naturalism, with reason trumping revelation. By incorporating modern scientific thinking into the Christian faith, liberalism veers into non-doctrinal thinking leading to a type of Christianity that is both relative and pluralistic.

I recommend further study of the information in the preceding footnote, especially Vogel and Becker for why the *historical-critical method* is so destructive to belief, as it gives a better understanding of the issues involved in higher criticism and the historical-critical method connected to it. It should be pointed out that society today believes strongly in the supernatural. In 2010 Greg Smith, a senior researcher for the Pew Forum on Religion and Public Life and author of "Religion Among the Millennials," stated that nearly 80 percent of all Americans believe in the supernatural during a National Public Radio broadcast of *Talk of the Nation* from NPR News. However, there is a huge gap between what the majority of Americans believe and what liberal Christian scholarship believes. It is disappointing that popular magazines and TV programs usually draw upon liberal Christian scholarship rather than conservative Christian scholarship.

The Jesus Seminar is comprised of liberal biblical scholars, most of whom have embraced the higher critical method of Bible interpretation. Even in the face of parallels today—where the dead are being raised, the blind see, the deaf hear, food is multiplied, and the audible voice of God is heard by key leaders—most of these scholars deny these realities as *a priori*—legends, myths, delusions at best, and fraudulent at worst.

The problem for these scholars is that these miracles, signs, and wonders *are* happening today. They are true. And not only are they true, but they are historical realities—actual events I have either personally witnessed or have personally interviewed the people who had the experiences or the families of those who had the experiences, including raising the dead. Once again the Messiah is fulfilling Isaiah 61, and sadly, once again religious authorities are rejecting His testimony.

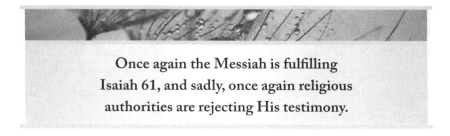

Once again the Messiah is fulfilling
Isaiah 61, and sadly, once again religious
authorities are rejecting His testimony.

The scholarly battle regarding the supernatural is still part of my pilgrimage to this day. It began many years ago when, as an eighteen-year-old, I walked into a college bookstore to purchase the required textbooks for my new major in Religious Studies. At that moment I heard a strong impression from the Holy Spirit that said, "The issue of your life will *be* the Holy Spirit." Later I would come to realize that the gifts of the Holy Spirit were also to be a big part of my life and ministry.

## DOES HEALING MINISTRY BELONG IN THE LIFE OF THE CHURCH TODAY?

Fast-forward forty-six years, to January 2016—I was in Norway as the keynote speaker for a seminar on healing at a Lutheran seminary. The issue to be addressed was, "Healing Ministry: Does It Belong in the Life of the Church and Its Congregations?" My two responders were also seminary professors. Our three lectures were followed by questions from a panel made up of one local pastor of a large Lutheran church, two other seminary professors, and another professor acting as moderator. I believe all of the professors who participated in the seminar are committed followers of Jesus Christ and that they all love His Church, and I am always grateful for an opportunity to discuss these issues in the context of a theological seminary, fully appreciating the work each has done in order to receive their degrees. I was especially grateful for the opportunity to share privately with one of the professors after the seminar. As we talked, I sensed his genuine desire to know God in a more intimate way and that God was at work in his questions and his concerns.

The first responder spoke on the use of the Bible for those dying of cancer. Her presentation was very critical of a theology that offered hope of healing rather than acceptance and reconciliation with death. From her perspective it was unethical for pastors to have a theology that hindered this acceptance. Though she primarily attacked the Word of Faith movement, there was nothing positive about the real possibility of healing from her point of view. It was clear from her presentation that her view on the question of whether the healing ministry belongs in the life of the Church and its congregations was a resounding *no!*

The next responder spoke on healing and deliverance ministry among Lutherans in Madagascar, accurately presenting the worldview of the people involved in that ministry. He was fair and sympathetic in his presentation. However, it was clear he questioned whether the worldview and theology of the ministers in Madagascar would transfer to the Norwegian context.

Though the topic of the seminar was whether or not healing ministry belonged in the life of the Church and its congregations, the panel failed to discuss any of the issues pertinent to having a healing ministry in the Church—issues such as how to establish a healing ministry, how to train a ministry team, and how to give oversight to ministry teams in local churches or in small groups. Instead, they approached healing as a theory, not a fact.

As I responded to the questions of the panel, I noticed that their questions were always preceded by a statement of concern regarding something I had said in my presentation or something I had written in my thesis. It was very clear that these professors were uncomfortable with the idea of a regular weekly ministry of healing as part of the life of the Church and its congregations.

Near the end of our time, the moderator asked me if I wasn't in something of a conundrum—a problem without a solution—because I criticized enlightenment thinking. To their way of understanding, enlightenment thinking had brought much good from the sciences and in the practice of medicine.

They cited as an example the fact that immunizations had been developed that save the lives of millions.

My response was that I too celebrated the advances in medical science, including the insights from psychosomatic medicine and the school of psychoneuroimmunology, which echoed much of the insight found in the New Testament regarding the positive effect of the fruit of the Spirit and the negative effect of the works of the flesh on the immune system. "Not everything in enlightenment thinking is a problem," I said. "Problems arise when we reduce reality to only that which can be scientifically verified, thus removing any belief in angels, demons, and for that matter even in God, although I do not include God in the negation of enlightenment thinking."

## ADRIAN'S HEALING

The real highlight of the seminar was the testimony of a woman named Marion. Marion's son Adrian was born with a rare disease that made it impossible for him to eat without becoming seriously ill. His digestive system was unable to draw nutrients from his food, making it necessary to feed him by tubal injection. In addition, Adrian had several others serious physical health problems. But all of that was history because Adrian had been completely and miraculously healed at Bethel Church in Redding, California. This healing took place when he was in his early teens. As I sat there among those skeptics who could find no place in their theology for the ministry of healing in the Church, I saw their arguments give way to tears of gratitude for the miraculous touch of our loving heavenly Father on one of His beloved sons. There was applause when Adrian stood up at the end of his mother's testimony. I have seen it over and over again—it's not apologetics that break through cessationist thinking; it is the manifest power of God as He lovingly touches a life that causes skepticism to give way to belief. Apologetics are part of the process, but real change comes when they are combined with the miraculous.

Liberal theology also has issues related to the dating of the gospels. Liberal commentators state that all the gospels had to have been written after A.D. 70, because Jesus' prediction as found in Matthew 24, Mark 13, and Luke 21—about the destruction of Jerusalem—is too accurate. To their way of thinking, Jesus' prediction must have been written back into the text after it happened.

Their method of dating the gospels is based upon their anti-supernatural understanding of reality[2] that does not allow for predictive prophecy.[3] This issue of the dating of the gospels is important because this strong anti-supernatural presupposition is the same presupposition that tries to explain away healings and miracles and reduce them to myths, legends, and embellishments or give them a naturalistic explanation.

## CESSATIONISM

Unlike liberalism, cessationism is typically very theologically conservative, holding fast to the doctrines of the Church while believing that the miracle gifts of the Holy Spirit—healing, tongues, and prophetic revelation—ceased with the end of the apostolic era, once the Church was established and the canon closed.[4] They believe that the purpose of miracles is evidential in relationship to correct doctrine.[5] Some cessationists hold fast to the belief that the gifts will not reemerge, while others assert that it is possible for God to occasionally perform miracles today as His sovereign answer to prayers and in those places where the Church is being established for the first time. The cessationist position is a violation of the biblical doctrine of the Kingdom of God and of the Holy Spirit's continuing role in the Church beyond His role in salvation, while also contradicting many Scriptures that teach that the gifts are to continue until Jesus' return.[6]

## NEO-ORTHODOXY

Next we have neo-orthodoxy, which emerged in the twentieth century primarily through theologians Karl Barth[7] and Emil Brunner. Very popular among seminaries in the twentieth century, neo-orthodoxy, while going in the opposite direction from liberalism, particularly regarding revelation, strenuously rejected healings and miracles, embracing some of liberalism's anti-supernatural presuppositions while being more conservative in its conclusions.[8] Though Barth, a reformed pastor and a cessationist, embraced revelation, his teachings on the subject were wanting and his theology leaned strongly toward universalism. Van Harvey, a liberal, had strong opinions that the neo-orthodox theologian Barth and others had violated the historical method.[9]

## DISPENSATIONALISM

Dispensationalism is a theology that asserts biblical history is to be interpreted based on a series of time periods or dispensations administered to the Church by God. Dispensational theology holds an ultra-pessimistic view of the Church in the end times and is the source of pre-tribulation theology. Pre-tribulation theology came to the Church first through Margaret MacDonald (Scotland, 1830) and was picked up by John Nelson Darby, an Anglican priest who founded the

Plymouth Brethren church, and later popularized by Scofield's Reference Bible (1909). Darby was a cessationist who held the dispensationalist view that Jesus will return for a weak Church. This pre-tribulation mindset leads to a type of religious neutralism that can have a paralyzing effect, causing Christians to withdraw from societal conflict in anticipation of Christ's imminent second coming, leaving no room for the victorious end-time Church that revival can bring.

## FUNDAMENTALISM

Fundamentalists, as we noted in Chapter 10, entered the scene as a backlash to liberal theology, whose heyday began when Darwin's theory of evolution was accepted as fact by many in the Church. Popularized by Princeton theologian B.B. Warfield's book *Counterfeit Miracles,*[10] which we examine in Chapter 14, the fundamentalist movement went head to head with modernist-liberals and lost on many fronts, not the least of which was the Scopes Trial of 1925.[11] Their reaction was to set up their own schools and insulate themselves from liberalism to the greatest extent possible. Remember, fundamentalists, like cessationists, believe that the miracle gifts are no longer in existence in the Church.

The modernist-fundamentalist controversy hit the American Church in the 1920s.[12] Conservatives, who believed the Bible is true historically, rose up in an attempt to regain control of the teaching institutions of the American Church but failed, leaving the majority of Christian colleges, divinity schools, and seminaries in the hands of liberals who proceeded to produce skeptical ministers who would reject any belief in the supernatural, both today and historically in the Bible,[13] refusing to believe the gifts of healings or working of miracles were for today.[14] Fundamentalists, while believing healing could occur, believed it was not due to the gift of healing but due to God sovereignly responding to the Church's intercessory prayer on behalf of the sick person, and these answers to prayer were not to be normative.[15]

Theologically speaking, the American and European Protestant churches were, and still are, the bastions of skepticism and unbelief concerning healing and miracles in the Church. My experience in university and seminary revealed our institutions of higher learning to be centers for skepticism rather than centers to strengthen faith, but thankfully things are slowly changing.

## THE FAITH CURE MOVEMENT

The exception to this scenario would arise in the nineteenth century in what is now called the Faith Cure movement. This healing movement believed that Jesus died for healing, as well as for forgiveness, and that this healing would be appropriated by believing the promises of the Bible concerning healing and then confessing these promises until they manifested in healing.[16] Some, Andrew Murray and A.B. Simpson specifically, discovered this truth through their own healing, and others, such as A. J. Gordon, Charles Cullis, and W.E. Boardman, discovered it through their study of the Bible.

The critical critique of the Faith Cure movement by Buckley and Warfield reaffirmed healing as a heresy and an illusion. Those who held strongly to healing prayer were labeled heretics, and the religious communities to which they belonged were deemed not really part of the Christian Church at all, but cults, and not worthy of study or valued as part of the Kingdom of God. Rather, any attention given to them would be of the curiosity nature, characterized by such things as sociology professors examining the ritual of snake handling.

Faith Cure movement survivors, the coming Pentecostal movement, and various miscellaneous Christian healing movements—such as the Camps Farthest Out (CFO), a summer retreat begun in the 1930s—were written out of the sweep of American Christian history and relegated to the category of cult and curiosity. This is demonstrated in the work of the prominent Christian scholar and historian of American Christianity, William Warren Sweet.[17] Neither the American Lutherans nor the Catholics received much coverage in spite of their large numbers. Pentecostals received no notice and, similarly, the Faith Cure movement was not mentioned. Paul Chappell, who wrote a thesis on the Faith Cure movement or, as he termed it, the divine healing movement, noted in 1983 how the Faith Cure had been written out of American church history.

The Pentecostal movement went beyond the understanding of the Faith Cure movement. Its followers believed in the restoration of the gifts of the Spirit, miracles, and the offices of the New Testament—apostles, prophets, evangelists, pastors, and teachers. Many of the early Pentecostals also agreed with the Faith Cure movement's negative view of medicine.[18] The popularity of this rediscovery of healing was short-lived, however, because its negative view of medicine led to needless deaths.[19] Although there were many positive attributes with this movement, ultimately its view on medicine was a negative position that hurt the healing movement and led to its demise.[20]

Healing was the most controversial subject of the Protestant Church during the last twenty-five years of the nineteenth century.[21] It is important to realize that, historically, the rediscovery of the doctrine of healing within historical Protestantism[22] did not originate with Pentecostals, because the Pentecostal movement would not begin until 1901. While healing later became identified as a Pentecostal doctrine, in reality it was rediscovered and developed by Evangelicals.[23]

> Healing was the most controversial subject
> of the Protestant Church during the last
> twenty-five years of the nineteenth century.

## NEW LIBERALISM

Last but not least of the movements within Protestant Christianity that have had a negative impact on the Church's belief and practice of healings and miracles is what we call *new* liberalism. More radical than liberalism, new liberalism seeks to *demythologize* Scripture. Rudolph Bultmann and Paul Tillich are considered the most prominent proponents of new liberalism. Tillich, a German-American theologian and philosopher who taught at Union Theological Seminary and then Harvard, enjoyed wide influence through his writings, public speaking and teaching. Bultmann, a German theologian and professor at the University of Marburg, became one of the foremost voices of liberal Christianity by reducing the miracles of the New Testament to myths or made-up stories that were intended to teach theological truths. To Bultmann's way of thinking, biblical stories don't have to be true in order to make their point. All we need do is embrace the truths revealed by the stories. This presupposition is extremely anti-supernatural.[24] This kind of radical rejection of the supernatural has wielded significant influence in the Church's perception and practice of healing.

# CHAPTER 13

# THE CHURCH REJECTS THE HOLY SPIRIT

Along with the various movements that had a negative impact on the practice of healing within the Church, it is important to understand the influences within Protestantism that led the Church away from healing. The outright rejection of the charismata by portions of the Church paints an unfortunate picture of the rejection of the person and presence of the precious Holy Spirit, the third person of the Trinity that Christ promised His Church (see John 16:1–15). While many who reject the gifts do not have any intention of rejecting the Holy Spirit, that is in essence what happens when they deny Him His proper place and function in the body of Christ. This rejection stems from fear, ignorance, and often the sinful nature of man reacting to the conviction the Spirit brings. Those in authority in the Church have historically shut down, defrocked, rejected, discriminated, fired, dis-fellowshipped, and isolated those persons through whom the Spirit is moving.

## ISSUES IN PROTESTANTISM

We will briefly examine some of the events in the history of the Protestant Church and some of the factors that I find are most prominent in this regard.

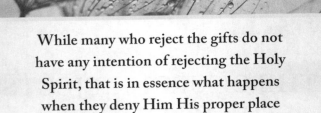

> While many who reject the gifts do not
> have any intention of rejecting the Holy
> Spirit, that is in essence what happens
> when they deny Him His proper place
> and function in the body of Christ.

### Johann Blumhardt Shut Down

Born in 1805 in Stuttgart, Germany, Lutheran theologian, teacher, and pastor Johann Blumhardt led one of the first modern-day healing revivals before being shut down by the church and the government. This revival sprang from a protracted deliverance by Blumhardt that played itself out in his Church over a period of two years. When the young woman was finally delivered, revival ensued, transforming the village and attracting those in need of healing and deliverance from the surrounding areas.[1] Healings and conversions abounded until nervous church officials finally ordered Blumhardt to cease and desist ministering in the supernatural. In 1853 Blumhardt left his pastorate in Wurttemberg and moved to a nearby village where he established a healing center.

### Edward Irving Defrocked

Scottish-born pastor Edward Irving ministered in the Presbyterian Church of Scotland in the mid-1800s before being called to pastor a church in London. Embracing teaching coming out of John McLeod Campbell's church in Scotland that the gifts of the Spirit had not ceased, Irving began to teach and preach on the Holy Spirit and the restoration of the gifts.[2] As his teachings took hold, parishioners began to experience the gifts of tongues and prophecy during regular Sunday morning services. These manifestations aroused the ire of church officials and a complaint was eventually filed against Irving that led to him being declared a heretic. In 1831 he was stripped of his ordination. Irving attempted to start his own church[3] where the gifts were allowed to flourish, but without a solid scriptural understanding of the gifts and their place and operation in the body of Christ, the church descended into chaos and eventually shut its doors. Irving died a tarnished man.

The lesson here, for those of us in the current Charismatic Renewal movement, and for the Church is that it is essential that we understand *and welcome* the person and presence of the Holy Spirit and His role in the life of the Church and all believers lest we risk discrediting and rejecting the third person of the Trinity and all that He brings.

### Pentecostal Movement Violently Rejected

In its earliest stages, the Pentecostal movement was most often associated with marginalized people groups. Healing evangelists helped spread the movement but were unable to lift it above the wave of violent rejection coming from mainline Christianity. Even the Holiness movement that gave birth to Pentecostalism would reject it, raising their voice more stridently and vehemently than anyone else save for a few of the later Holiness denominations that went Pentecostal.[4] Respected theologians would dub revivals such as Azusa Street "the last vomit of Satan,"[5] and characterized those who participated as "Satan's preachers, jugglers, necromancers, enchanters, magicians, and all sorts of mendicants."[6] Fiery feminist Alma Bridwell White's tirade[7] against the Pentecostal practice of tongues is representative of the view held by many in the Church regarding the manifestations of the supernatural.

## Much Tension Still Exists

Gradually Pentecostalism began to find acceptance within the Church and eventually gave rise to the current global renewal movements we see around the world today; although, as we have seen, much tension still exists within the Church regarding the restoration of the charismatic gifts. Until quite recently, many Bible colleges and seminaries discriminated against Pentecostals and Charismatics, refusing them entrance if they spoke in tongues. Protestant mission boards continue to fire Charismatic missionaries who do not adhere to cessationist theology,[8] and mainline denominations dis-fellowship churches that experience and express charismatic gifts.[9] Even those denominations that do accept the charismatic often marginalize it by relegating charismatic fellowship to off-hours worship that must meet outside the main sanctuary. It does not help that the movement has been tainted by prominent leaders who have suffered very public gross moral failures. While scandalous behavior is found throughout the Church, when it rears its head within the renewal movement it quickly becomes fodder for critics.

## ISSUES IN CATHOLICISM

While the Protestant Church was struggling through issues regarding the ministry of healing and the miraculous, the Catholic Church also wrestled with issues surrounding the ministry of healing. For centuries, from the ninth century to the mid-1500s, the institution of the Catholic Church was a blend of church and state, rendering church authority prey to the ambitious and powerful. The political authority of the day was duty bound to support the Church, which in turn reinforced the authority of those in government. The monarchies of Europe existed hand in hand with the Catholic Church, standing together to maintain social equilibrium and promote political unity, with great moral and political corruption abounding. From the 1500s to the twenty-first century, the Catholic Church underwent a gradual separation of Church and state and all of the internal upheaval that accompanied that paradigm shift.

Catholic and Protestant theology share common beliefs concerning the doctrine of the Trinity, the deity and humanity of Jesus Christ, the crucifixion of Christ, and the virgin birth. While I will in no way attempt to go into a study of Catholic theology here or Catholic versus Protestant theology, I want to very briefly highlight some of the more prominent ways in which the Catholic Church, like its Protestant counterpart, rejected the ministry of healing. It is important to note that the two major versions of Christianity in the world have historically neglected the ministry of healing, although the Catholics to a somewhat lesser extent than Protestants. For example, the ministry of deliverance has been practiced more strenuously by the Catholic Church, historically, than by the Protestant Church. Today we are seeing a resurgence of deliverance ministry in both the Catholics and Protestants. It should be pointed out that the Orthodox are Catholic, but not Roman Catholic, and would normally prefer the distinction of Orthodox. Since the first century they have believed in healing and even today have a liturgy for healing in their traditions. However, they don't emphasize healing or practice healing like the Pentecostals and Charismatics,[10] who are best known for healing.

Pertinent to our study are three factors within Catholic theology that combined to steer Catholicism away from faith in healing. First was an interpretation of healings, miracles, and dead raisings as the primary evidence of the deity of Christ instead of the expression of the gospel and the goodness of God as the primary purpose of miracles and healings. The evidential function should have been seen as a secondary purpose, not the primary.[11]

Second was a failure to distinguish between the context of Paul and Jesus' references to suffering—where suffering refers to persecution and tribulation because of one's faith—and the later reinterpretation of these texts as suffering referring to sickness, which was mistakenly seen as carrying one's cross, and glorifying Jesus in our suffering. Francis MacNutt does an excellent job of explaining how this was not a true biblical perspective, and one that needed correction in the theology of the Catholic layperson in order for more faith in healing to occur.[12] Note the similarity here to the extreme asceticism of mysticism mentioned earlier, which was not confined to the Catholic Church but also found in other Orthodox traditions.

The third Catholic theological factor was Augustine of Hippo's move away from the warfare worldview to a blueprint worldview. Prior to Augustine, and for a few hundred years after him, the predominant worldview held by the Church was that the forces of evil were at war against Christ and His Church.[13] This was viewed as *the* cause for the sicknesses and demonic bondage people experienced. In the warfare worldview, the Holy Spirit's power is to be used to fight and resist sickness and disease as well as demonic oppression. The enormous influence of Augustine's writings, which eventually became foundational in both Catholic and Protestant theology, helped move the Church to the "blueprint" worldview, which believes that everything happens due to the predetermined will of God. The problem with this worldview is that if God ordains everything, then He is responsible for evil, including sickness. If that is the case, instead of praying for healing the tendency is to pray for discernment to determine why God has brought this sickness into someone's life.[14]

Augustine's *writings* introduced the concept of reason over revelation, strongly influencing Thomas Aquinas' *Summa Theologica* and giving the Catholic Church its own version of rationalism. Synthesizing Aristotelian philosophy with Christian theology, the writings of Aquinas became especially influential among the Dominicans and the Jesuits. It is of note that Aristotelianism was much earlier particularly influential among Islamic scholars. This made Aquinas' teachings useful in the Catholic Church's attempts to Christianize the Arab world.[15]

The fourth Catholic theological factor that contributed to the demise of miracles and healings was Jerome's translation of James 5:14-15, where he translated the Greek word *sōzō* as "save" rather than "heal." This small yet significant revision in translation led to a change in the sacrament of Last Rights (Extreme Unction).[16] Instead of praying for a person's healing, the focus shifted to forgiveness to prepare the person for death.

Each of these factors and many others contributed to steer the Catholic Church away from the ministry of healing. Is it any wonder that as the two bastions of Christianity—Catholicism and Protestantism—inadvertently drew alongside one another in stiff-arming the ministry of healing, the Church as a whole almost succeeded in relegating healings and miracles to the dustbin?

## A HEALING AWAKENING

George L. Carey, 103rd Archbishop of Canterbury, in his Foreword to Bishop John Howe's book, *Anointed by the Spirit*, says this:

> History reveals that theories about the Spirit have abounded through the centuries leading to confusion as well as division. At the Reformation divisions in the Western Church led the Catholic Church to focus the Spirit's activity in the Church and particularly through its ministry, sacraments and life. Similarly, the Reformation churches limited the Spirit's role to the scriptures and effective preaching. While this is an oversimplification, these two trends remained the norm until the Pentecostal movement of the twentieth century blew apart this seriously flawed sacramental/scriptural divide to introduce the notion of the Spirit as the ever active, personal, dynamic in the life of every believer.[17]

Now, in the twenty-first century , thanks to those who have come before us to champion the place of the Spirit in the life of the Church and all believers, winds of change are blowing through the Church to a much greater extent than many in the Western Church realize. Churches in Asia, like those in Africa and Latin America, are very open to healing. In fact, healing is one of the reasons churches are growing so fast worldwide. I see this happening as I travel the globe preaching and teaching and ministering. As this book gets ready to go to press, I have just returned from two back-to-back conferences, one in Bangkok and the other in Singapore. There were thousands in attendance at each conference from some thirty nations, most from Asia, with hundreds of healings and salvations.

The explosive church growth we are seeing worldwide mirrors the explosive growth that the first-century Church experienced, and it is largely because of the miraculous. Those first-century converts to Christianity were typically coming out of the rampant paganism of their day. It was not just wise and good teaching that opened their eyes to the person and presence of Jesus Christ, but the healings and miracles and deliverances that occurred along with the teaching. The first-century Church had no Bible. There was no biblical text on which to base their theology. They were living what was to become the biblical text. It was the manifest presence and power of God through the miraculous that drew people to Christianity, and it is happening again today because many who are coming to Christ have their own "bible" and their own "theology." Our Christian theology carries no weight with them. It is the power and presence of God that draws them to Himself.

Several years ago I was in Minneapolis-St. Paul conducting a school of healing and impartation. Our hosting church was a 5,000-member Lutheran church. Many were touched in this conference. Two of those touched were a husband and wife couple—Mark and Tammy. Mark and Tammy received such a powerful impartation of the Holy Spirit that they ended up closing their very successful business to go on staff at their church in preparation for missionary work in Malaysia. Several years later I had the privilege of meeting Mark and Tammy at a conference in Australia. They had flown down from Malaysia hoping to receive a fresh touch from God. The stories they began to share with me from their ministry work in Malaysia were almost beyond belief. In fact, I'm sure they would be unbelievable for those who do not embrace a present-day ministry of the Holy Spirit with signs and wonders that follow the preaching of the gospel.

> It was not just wise and good teaching
> that opened their eyes to the person
> and presence of Jesus Christ, but the
> healings and miracles and deliverances
> that occurred along with the teaching.

At great risk to their lives, Mark and Tammy have been ministering the gospel to the Malay people, which is against the law. Under Malaysian law you can evangelize the Chinese and other ethnic groups in Malaysia, but not the Malay people who are Muslim. Like the apostle Paul, Mark and Tammy have been imprisoned for preaching the gospel. One story in particular stands out for me.

In one of the villages in the interior of the country, Mark and Tammy had developed a friendship with the person responsible for making sure that no Muslims convert to Christianity. This person's mother became very ill, and when Mark heard about her illness he offered to pray for her healing. At first the person was defensive and refused Mark's offer, but Mark felt led to press in, reminding his friend that now was not the time to argue religion. Finally the friend relented and agreed to let Mark come and pray. When Mark arrived at the mother's house, his friend was there along with a few other relatives. Mark prayed for the mother's healing, but nothing happened and finally he left, discouraged and confused as to why she was not healed.

A few days later Mark received a phone call from his friend who was now more desperate than before and quite angry. Not long after Mark had prayed for his mother, she had become much worse and been hospitalized. Now the family was angry that this Christian had been allowed to pray over their mother. They believed that demons had come to afflict their mother as a result of Mark's prayers, and they were blaming him for her deteriorating condition. A large number of family members had gathered in her hospital room, believing she was close to death.

Upon hearing all this, Mark again felt led by the Holy Spirit to go and pray for her, even though he was well aware of the gravity of a Christian praying for a Muslim. Not wanting to disobey the Holy Spirit, but a bit confused, he prayed, "Lord, I felt like you led me to pray for her in the village and nothing happened. Now they are blaming me for her worsening condition. Why didn't you heal her when I prayed?" Receiving no answer but knowing he must be obedient, he headed to the hospital.

When he reached the mother's room he found it full of her relatives, with many overflowing into the hallway. One of the relatives was a Malaysian police officer who had the authority to arrest Mark if he prayed for this Muslim woman. He knew ministering to a Malay was a serious violation of the law, yet he also knew that he was doing the will of God at that moment and so he asked for permission to pray. To this day he doesn't understand why this angry, grieving Muslim family allowed him to pray for their mother, but they did. And this time, when

Mark prayed the mother was healed right there in front of so many of her family.

Later, as Mark was leaving the hospital the Holy Spirit spoke to him again, saying, "I didn't heal her the first time because I had a better plan. If I had healed her the first time only a few of her family would have known it. By waiting until she was surrounded by scores of her family, I have brought greater honor and glory to My name, and many more than otherwise would will become my children." Mark told me that he was able to lead several members of this family to Jesus as a result of this healing.

The words of Friedrich Zündel, from his book *The Awakening: One Man's Battle with Darkness*,[18] exemplify the faith that has characterized those called to the ministry of healing throughout the history of the Church. We are seeing the fruit of that persevering faith today.

Blumhardt never doubted that this renewal would come, or that it was worth fighting for. He had tasted victory, and through him many others had too. What God gave one village through one man who turned to him, he wants to give the entire world. Möttlingen's triumph over darkness should give us courage to face our own demons, and hope to expect greater things to come. We are a dehydrated people. Nothing will quench our thirst and end the drought but God pouring out his spirit once again. Only a fraction of the promise was fulfilled at the time of the apostles. Must it not now be fulfilled on a larger scale? This stream of the Spirit will come—let us await it with confidence. The thirst is almost killing us, and people are deteriorating both inwardly and outwardly. But now, because we need this spirit, God will give it again.

God *is* giving His Spirit to us again, because we are in great need and because He loves us. I see it all over the world. We must be faithful to continue to press forward.

# CHAPTER 14

# CESSATIONISM: A BRIEF EXAMINATION OF THE TEACHINGS OF B.B. WARFIELD

Before we conclude our brief study of the reasons behind the decline of healing in the Church, an examination of the great teacher of cessationism, B.B. Warfield, and his work entitled *Counterfeit Miracles* is in order. Warfield's cessationist exposition is based upon three arguments. The first argument forms the foundation of his view on cessationism, while his second and third arguments are his pillars. Warfield sees the purpose of miracles as being evidential. They are to either vindicate or establish correct doctrine. This is why, according to cessationists, only the apostles were able to work miracles.

The problem with Warfield's foundational argument is that the true purpose of miracles is to express the gospel. Miracles are part of the good news that the Kingdom of God is at hand and that Jesus is the initiator of the Kingdom of God. Miracles, healings, and signs and wonders done by the disciples down to this day testify to the truth of the gospel by confirming the in-breaking of the Kingdom of God in the coming of Jesus.

The good news is that this power is available to all believers in Jesus to destroy the works of the devil and advance the Kingdom of God. Miracles were not to be relegated to the writers of Scripture. To believe only apostles could work miracles is a contradiction of Scripture.

Jon Ruthven reveals the weakness of Warfield's argument by pointing out the following. First, only three or four of the apostles wrote any Scripture. Almost 50 percent of the New Testament was written by non-apostles.[1] Second, the apostles were not the only ones who performed miracles in the Bible. Two of the first deacons did as well, so why should we not assume that all of the deacons performed miracles, as the Bible does not explicitly state that all of the twelve apostles performed miracles? Warfield's foundation is broken and will not sustain the weight of his argument.[2]

> Miracles are part of the good news that the
> Kingdom of God is at hand and that Jesus
> is the initiator of the Kingdom of God.

Warfield places no emphasis upon the fact that Philip and Steven moved in signs and wonders, as did unnamed persons in the Corinthian and Galatian churches. We find people called "workers of miracles," and another group noted as having "gifts of healing." First Corinthians 12:28 states, "And in the church God has appointed first of all apostles, second prophets, third teachers, then workers of miracles, also those having gifts of healing, those able to help others, those with gifts of administration, and those speaking in different kinds of tongues." Acts 8:5-6 states, "Philip went down to a city in Samaria and proclaimed the Christ there. When the crowds heard Philip and saw the miraculous signs he did, they all paid close attention to what he said." Acts 6:8 reads, "Now Stephen, a man full of God's grace and power, did great wonders and miraculous signs among the people." Also, when the Church was scattered and fled Jerusalem, unnamed Christians appear to have been used of God in signs and wonders, miracles and/ or healings, especially at Antioch.[3] Not to mention Ananias who prayed for Saul in Antioch.[4]

When examining the pillars of Warfield's historical argument and his biblical argument, his historical argument seems to be broken because it applies a different historical approach to biblical history than it does to post-biblical history. Warfield was a fundamentalist and, as such, criticized liberals in their denial of the miraculous events of the Bible. Warfield accepted the testimony of the biblical writers or their research of eyewitnesses. Liberals did not, because they were influenced by the rationalism of the Enlightenment and the arguments of Conyers Middleton and later David Hume's writings.[5]

When it came to the post-biblical, historical accounts of miracles, Warfield used tools and arguments that liberals had used on the Bible. He used an internally inconsistent and contradictory historical method, which if applied to biblical miracles would mean an acceptance of post-biblical miracles as well. Likewise, if Warfield were to apply his post-biblical, historical method to the Bible, he would have to deny the miracles of the Bible.[6]

Warfield's biblical pillar is also broken because it is inconsistent in its approach and actually violates his principles of

interpretation. When applying Warfield's principles of interpretation, one has to come to the understanding that the gifts
of the Spirit are to continue as long as they fulfill their purpose, which was to express the gospel. When one applies the
same historical method, there is no reason not to believe healings and miracles have continued throughout the history of the
Church and that the Bible actually teaches this through many
texts. In addition, the doctrine of the Holy Spirit's continued
ministry and the doctrine of the Kingdom of God clearly teach
the importance of the continuation of the charismata.[7]

# PART SIX

# RECLAIMING OUR AUTHORITY TO HEAL

*Then the eleven disciples went to Galilee, to the mountain where Jesus had told them to go. When they saw him, they worshiped him; but some doubted. Then Jesus came to them and said, "All authority in heaven and on earth has been given to me. Therefore go and make disciples of all nations, baptizing them in the name of the Father and of the Son and of the Holy Spirit, and teaching them to obey everything I have commanded you. And surely I am with you always, to the very end of the age" (Matthew 28:16-20).*

# CHAPTER 15

# THE HEALING RIVER OF GOD

## TIMES OF REVIVAL

Based on the cessationist argument, it might sound like the Church went for centuries without any faith in or practice of the supernatural gifts of the Holy Spirit, but that is far from the truth. The power of God has continued throughout the centuries in seasons of ebb and flow. Perhaps the greatest period of "flow" came following the Day of Pentecost and continued through the first 300 or 400 years of recorded church history. Then, following the Middle Ages and the Reformation, there seemed to be a significant "ebb" to the power of God, namely because of the widespread embrace of reason and intellectualism at the expense of the supernatural.

## SIGNS OF RESTORATION

Evangelicals began seeing healings in the mid-1800s, and from 1875 until 1900 healing was the most controversial subject of many denominations. God was revealing Himself in supernatural power in the midst of the most conservative, mainline denominations. Many of today's cessation-teaching churches were birthed in renewal movements marked by charismatic manifestations.[1]

## Baptist Revival

In 1994, when I heard the president of the Southern Baptist Convention state that the Baptists had had many periods of revival and that none of them had the manifestations that were occurring in Toronto, I had my secretary contact each of the seminaries in the Convention to speak to their professors of evangelism. When they were asked by phone, "What was the greatest revival in Baptist history?" the response was unanimously, "The Shantung Revival in China."

Because healing, falling or being slain in the Spirit, feeling "electricity," laughing in the Spirit, and even raising the dead are recorded in *The Shantung Revival*—a book by Mary Crawford, one of the Southern Baptist missionaries who experienced this revival firsthand in the early 1930s—the statement by the president of the Southern Baptist Convention is simply incorrect. Crawford's book is almost entirely comprised of letters written by Southern Baptist missionaries to each other in China during the Shantung Revival. Unfortunately, most Southern Baptists are not aware of what happened during their greatest revival. Around 1970, the book was reprinted with almost all of the phenomena of the Holy Spirit edited out by a Southern Baptist official. Global Awakening has republished Mary Crawford's book with its entire original content.[2]

## The Pentecostal Revival

Just as the 1800s were ushered in by revival, so were the 1900s. The Frontier Revival, or Second Great Awakening as it was called, was followed a century later by the even more powerful Pentecostal Revival, which dates back to 1901. Like the Second Great Awakening, in the Pentecostal Revival people once again experienced manifestations such falling, shaking, rolling, weeping, wailing, dancing, laughing in the Spirit, and speaking in tongues.[3] What was unique about the Pentecostal Revival was that for the first time speaking in tongues was tied to the baptism of the Holy Spirit as the initial evidence, though initially this was not the primary Pentecostal position that it later developed into. Also, divine healing became a doctrinal position of Pentecostal denominations.

### Azusa Street

Azusa Street occurred in 1906 and was initially called the *Los Angeles Blessing*.[4] Hungry people traveled from every inhabited continent to find more of the manifest presence of God. Participants believed in impartation and the transference of anointing, empowering them to carry the revival back to other places.[5] One of the major traits of this revival was divine healing, which seemed to also be transferable through impartations of the Holy Spirit.

Like the subsequent Latter Rain Revival of the 1940s, Azusa Street emphasized the restoration of all the spiritual gifts of First Corinthians 12, including the so-called *"sign gifts"* of tongues, interpretation of tongues, prophecy, working miracles, and gifts of healings. Today, however, healing is seen as the most characteristic distinguishing mark of Pentecostalism according to Brown and Lederle.[6]

## THE FULLNESS OF OUR SALVATION

It is disappointing to see how much prejudice still exists in the Church today toward Pentecostals. I see this prejudice as due to the threat that Pentecostalism poses to the doctrine of cessationism that has permeated the Protestant denominations, primarily from the emphasis upon healing by the new

Pentecostal denominations. Gifts of healings and working of miracles still in existence today among the Pentecostals threaten to undermine the whole doctrine of cessationism.

As a young man, when I took a course on evangelism in seminary, all revivals in North American church history were studied except three: the Pentecostal Revival, the Latter Rain Revival—which was a Pentecostal revival in its origin—and the Charismatic renewal.[7] The Charismatic renewal had only recently ended, and the Jesus Movement was still happening. The Jesus Movement was not studied either. It is shameful that these revivals are not mentioned in some of the evangelical seminaries and colleges today.[8] It is not healthy to allow our prejudice to blind us to the facts of how powerfully God has used Pentecostals in recorded history.

In their early days, when they had no institutions, buildings, money, or programs, God used Pentecostals to reach more lost people than any other part of the Church—more than the Reformed, the Lutherans, the Anglicans, the Baptists, the Methodists, and the Catholics. These historical classic denominations—with all their history, buildings, finances, organization, and programs—were surpassed in evangelism by the Pentecostals. Why? Because Pentecostals embraced the outpouring of the Holy Spirit's power and the restoration of the power ministries of the Holy Spirit as still for today, especially the gifts of healing, working of miracles, and deliverance.

*Sozo*, the Greek word for "save," is used in the Bible to refer to not only the saving of the soul but, more often, for deliverance from demonization and physical and emotional healing. It was this understanding of the fullness of our salvation, embraced by the Pentecostals, that gave such spiritual power to their message.

## THE COMPASSION OF GOD

Pentecostalism was preceded by forerunner leaders such as Charles Spurgeon (1834–1892) who were looking for the restoration of a fully-empowered, apostolic Church as seen in the days of the first Pentecost. Spurgeon was a Calvinist, yet he had a healing ministry and moved in words of knowledge during his services.[9] He was not a "healing evangelist." The focus of his ministry was the grace, compassion, and truth of God found in the Bible. His ministry of healing was based totally on his understanding of the compassion of God toward his children.

Mr. Spurgeon, like the Master (Jesus) whom he so faithfully served, went about teaching and healing the sick. He never took any credit for himself for the healing power that he exercised. Hundreds of people physically benefited from his visits, many of whom he never afterward directly heard from. He regarded himself, as every pastor should, as a mere agent of divine power and spoke of himself, in two instances, as unworthy of possessing the gift of healing.[10]

He prophesied a great move of the Holy Spirit in the next fifty years,[11] and it was in those next fifty years that the birth of the Holiness Movement occurred, spearheaded by some leading Methodists, with its first holiness call back to revivalism and sanctification.

## THE HOLINESS AND
## FAITH-CURE MOVEMENTS

The first holiness camp meeting was held in 1867 by northern Methodist leaders. Later, non-Methodists,[12] who were beginning another movement called the Faith Cure movement, would begin to have an impact on the Holiness meetings with their emphasis upon healing.[13] The Faith Cure movement was one of the most controversial movements of the last quarter of the nineteenth century, and the majority of Christians today know little about it.

The holiness movement emphasized a second work of grace following initial regeneration. The purpose of this second experience was a "filling" with the power of the Holy Spirit, which enabled the believer to experience sanctification—practical victory in his daily experience, not just positional victory in the spiritual realm and the life to come. It was a return to the doctrine of "Christ is Victor" (*Christus Victor*), which was the prevailing understanding of the cross of Christ during the first 1,000 years of church history.[14] In short, it means we understand that the cross did not just secure our ultimate salvation but that all of Satan's power was met head-on and defeated, breaking the dominion of the curse.

The death of Jesus was certainly a "substitutionary atonement," but the scope of what He did goes far beyond that. By His death and resurrection, Jesus conquered all the powers of hell. Because of Jesus' victory, Christians may walk in authority and power over death in all its forms—spiritual, emotional, and physical.[15]

Out of this return to historic *Christus Victor* theology came the Faith Cure movement. This movement would be eclipsed in about twenty-five years by the birth of the Pentecostal movement.[16] There would be more than twenty-five new Pentecostal denominations founded during the first twenty-five years of the twentieth century.[17] With the great disdain of evangelical Protestants for the Pentecostal movement, which embraced healing, there was a reaction by Evangelicals away from the

Faith Cure movement into an even stronger cessationist position. The members of the newly developed "Fundamentalists" were adamantly against healing and Pentecostalism.[18]

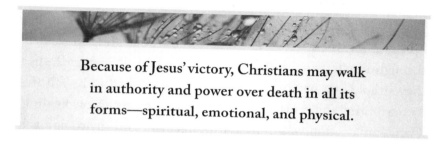

Because of Jesus' victory, Christians may walk in authority and power over death in all its forms—spiritual, emotional, and physical.

## MANIFESTATIONS OF SUPERNATURAL POWER CONTINUE

Can there be any question that the mightiest moves of the Spirit that have resulted in the greatest numbers of people coming to God have been those times of revival characterized by powerful outpourings of spiritual gifts and manifestations of God's very presence? Yet the Church has been more concerned with phenomena than with evangelism. There has been so much opposition to the phenomena that the critics could not value the fruit of evangelism that accompanied the power of the Holy Spirit.

What is clear from church history is that most of its Charismatic leaders first received their own impartation of the Spirit prior to accomplishing powerful works in Jesus' name. Men and women like Maria Woodworth-Etter, John G. Lake, Smith Wigglesworth, Charles Price, F.F. Bosworth, Aimee Semple-McPherson, Tommy Hicks, Lester Sumrall, T.L. Osborne, Oral Roberts, Kathryn Kuhlmann, Reinhard Bonnke, Benny Hinn, Bill Johnson, Leif Hetland, Heidi Baker, myself, and a host of others all received a powerful impartation from God before we were so powerfully used of God.

Other men like A.J. Gordon, Andrew Murray, A.B. Simpson, E.W. Kenyon, A.T. Pierson, D.L. Moody, and R.A. Torrey also testified to having received the baptism in the Holy Spirit. These men were less connected to the healing movement through impartation, much like the late John Wimber. Rather, they simply saw healing in the Bible and wanted to be faithful to Scripture, and to that end they began teaching on healing. Their impartation was more for evangelism, and their approach to healing was based upon the promises of Scripture.[19]

When we see men and women who claim an anointing of God to move in signs and wonders, healings and deliverance and see ministries accompanied by all manner of phenomena, can we clearly discern whether or not it is of God? Church history reveals the impact of men and women used in the past and the fruit of earlier outpourings of the Spirit. But what about more recent times?

## THE RIVER OF GOD'S POWER CONTINUES TO FLOW

Like many streams flowing into one great river of God, the 1940s brought the healing revival ministry of William Branham in 1946, the Sharon Orphanage Revival of 1947, the Healing Revival of 1948, and the evangelistic ministry of Billy Graham in 1949. Although diverse in nature, I do not believe these were separate moves of God, but one great outpouring that manifested in a variety of ways. Since then, there has been acceleration toward the greatest revival of all—the last harvest before the return of Jesus Christ in the consummation of

His Kingdom. Whether I will live to see this or whether it is another 100 years away, time is moving toward the consummation of the Kingdom of God.

The great River of God revival of the mid-1990s is similar in nature to the late 1940s revival, which was made up of many streams. In the 1990s, there was Claudio Freidzon (Argentina, 1992), Rodney Howard-Browne (from South Africa and the outpouring in Lakeland, Florida in 1993), John Arnott and myself (Toronto, 1994), John Kilpatrick and Steve Hill (Pensacola, Florida, 1995), and Steve Gray (Smithton, Missouri, 1996). During this time there was also an outpouring of the Spirit upon Christian colleges and universities. There are many others who were used in these periods of revival both in the 1940s and the 1990s. These revivals were not only characterized by manifestations or phenomena of the Holy Spirit, but also by the gifts of the Holy Spirit, especially healing.

In this last decade evangelists Benny Hinn and Reinhard Bonnke have preached to millions in one location. I was ministering in India during the time that Benny Hinn was ministering there. He was drawing crowds of a million; my crowds were from 25,000 to 100,000 per night. What drew the people? *The miracles of God drew them!*

Evangelist Billy Graham does not move in miracles in his ministry, and yet I do not believe his success invalidates my arguments. Even though his ministry is not a "miracles" ministry per se, it nonetheless impacts people evangelistically by the power of the Holy Spirit. In his autobiography, Billy Graham tells of the time he went up in the mountains of California near a lake, where he had an experience with God.[20] It was there that he made a more complete surrender to the purposes and power of God for his life. This experience happened shortly before his famous 1949 Los Angeles meetings, which brought him national notoriety. In 1946, about three years prior to this experience in the mountains and before the overwhelming responses to his crusades, Billy Graham was filled with the Holy Spirit. This came about as a result of his meeting and friendship with Stephen Olford, who talked to him about being filled with the Spirit. What followed was an intense time of study and seeking by Billy Graham. The result was that Graham and Olford prayed together for such an experience in Billy Graham's life,[21] which God gave him. It was after this infilling of the Holy Spirit that we see Graham's ministry increasing exponentially.

There are so many more men and women who have been powerfully anointed by God to bring about revival through the various gifts of the Spirit. You can find some of their stories in my book *There Is More*,[22] which tells how the Lord of the Church brought the doctrines of impartation, gifts of healings, and working of miracles from the brink of extinction to a full-blown massive recovery effort orchestrated by the Holy Spirit. So much more has happened even since I wrote that book and since the publication of the revised edition. It is nothing short of astounding to discover how significant this move of God, with its recapturing the gifts of the Spirit, has been to the growth of the Church since 1901.

# A NEW PENTECOST

The Church of God—the Church of our Lord Jesus Christ in all of its many streams—is beginning to see a restoration of all of the early gifts. I see this as I travel the world. The testimonies are increasing daily. Here is a testimony from Nazarene evangelist Dan Bohi that will give you courage to believe for this new Pentecost.

> I had an encounter with Jesus in 1995. I had a car wreck where I was hit by a semi. I was in a hospital bed for a year. Jesus came to my bed, and that is when I was filled with the Spirit. Ever since then I've been sensitive to the Spirit.
>
> In 2008, after losing a lot of money in the housing crash, I asked God what to do with my life and he said to read the Bible. So I read the whole Bible, and he called me to wake up to the power, purity, and freedom in the Spirit-filled life. I got a call to go to the churches. That was October 10, 2008. Since that time—it has been six years and ten months— I've been to 712 churches. I've seen about 38,000 physical healings and over 155,000 people have come forward to be baptized in the Holy Spirit. I don't have formal training or education.

God told me three things when he called me. He said, "Read the Bible every month," so for the first six years I read the Bible every thirty days so that the Word would become flesh in my heart. After that God said, "Get prayer support and let the superintendents and pastors send out testimonies."

So I'm going along doing this and everything is great. About three years ago, the Holy Spirit started telling me that the reason we are sanctifying is so that heaven can come to earth, so I started preaching on gifts. Then, I got your book, *There is More!* I read it five times (now I've read it seven times), and that is what was happening—people being touched by the Spirit flowing through me.

I had never even heard of impartation. I had a dream that revival broke out, and it was seven nights a week on GodTV. People came from every nation. I woke up on Friday morning from that dream, and that is the day you prayed for impartation over the phone with me.

The next thirty days after that impartation prayer were busy days. The first church that I went to was in Waco, Texas. I got a word of knowledge that someone's stomach was being healed. I spoke the word before my sermon. After my sermon, a lady was red in the face, and I thought she was having a heart attack. She said, "I can't believe what is happening." She had been deaf her whole life, and now she could hear. My wife told me that we got a letter from the lady who ran the sound booth at that church. She had a nine-year stomach disorder, and she was instantly healed when I spoke that word of knowledge. That was the first church after your call.

The next church was in Wichita Falls, Texas. A lady asked me to pray for her five-year-old boy who had asthma. The Holy Spirit said, "Pray for his eyes." I kept praying for people, and the little kid told his mom that he didn't need his glasses. He ran out of the sanctuary. His mom testified that he could see perfectly. His asthma and his eyes were healed.

The next church was in Iron, Texas. I used one of my services to do whatever the Holy Spirit said to do. This one guy stood up, and I knew him. He had Parkinson's disease and he had never been healed. He came walking down front. He said, "The Lord told me to stand up." When he stood up, electricity went through his body. He held his hands up, and it was the first time his hands weren't shaking. All he did was stand up, and the Holy Spirit went through him and took away his Parkinson's.

In Denison, Texas I felt opposition, like spiritual warfare. I asked if anyone felt demonized. A pastor's wife fell on the ground, so pastors put their hands on her to cast the demon out. Another woman came forward who was eight and a half months pregnant and had arm braces on because she had nerve damage. I prayed for her; she turned around and took four steps away from me and started crying, then took her arm braces off and moved her hands, which she hadn't been able to do in two years. She was instantly healed.

Then I went from there to Athens, Texas. There was a black lady who had a boot on one of her legs. She said her Achilles tendon was not fused to her heal bone. She had diabetes, and she had three procedures but they couldn't get her tendon to fuse. We prayed for her, I turned around and she took her boot off. The next day she got an x-ray from her doctor. Her x-ray had a note from her doctor that says, "There is no explanation for this, the bone is fused."

The next service I went to was in Gilmore, Texas. The pastor there had five crushed discs from military service, 22 years in the Navy. He was not emotional, but he got really emotional. He bent over and touched the ground, which he hadn't been able to do in fourteen years. Another guy named Jimmy, who was blind nine years, we prayed for him and that night his eyesight came back after nine years.

This all happened the month after you prayed that impartation. They were all churches in Texas, all Nazarene churches. Then I went to Odessa, Texas. A lady came up to me with a walker before the service and said she has neuropathy. She couldn't feel her legs. She was 70 years old and asked me to pray for her husband. I wanted to pray for her, but she said to pray for her husband because he was a Christian but he was not "all in." I prayed for him for three days, and he stared at me like he was skeptical. I laid hands on the wife the third day. She went out in the Spirit, and she was healed of her neuropathy. Her husband came to the altar and got up and hugged me and apologized for being skeptical and said he was "all in."

Then I went to Belton, Texas and a couple of retired superintendents came forward. A guy named Marcel had stage IV cancer in his chest. I put my hand on his chest and he felt electricity go through his chest. The next week, his son who teaches Sunday school told me that his dad's stage IV tumor was gone.

The final church I went to was in Woodland, Texas. I was struggling with a bit of fear because of criticism I got on the Internet. I wanted to go home and take a break. I called my wife, and she said, "You can't come home." So that afternoon the Holy Spirit came into my car and asked me if I was going to stay in fear or get back into the Kingdom. That night I had peace while ministering. I was praying for people, and a couple of people fell on the ground. I was blessing some folks. A man came up to me after the service and said he needed to talk to me. He said, "When you touched me tonight when I came forward, a bright light came over me, and I was blinded. I was stuck in God's hand. I saw the light come on me, and then God's hands grabbed me, and I couldn't see or hear anything but God, and he told me to bless your ministry." This man now gives my ministry $100,000 a year.

Here's my last story. I was in Columbus, Ohio. I laid hands on a lady named Melissa. Four days later, she called from the doctor's office, and her dead fetus had come back to life. She was at the doctor scheduling her DNC, and her dead fetus came back to life. That is the sixth time I've seen that happen in my ministry. That was the last weekend of April 2015.

I believe God is breathing upon His whole Church, across all denominational lines, awakening all of us to His power and authority and bringing unity to the body—an ecumenism of the Spirit rather than doctrinal ecumenism. I believe that the recovery of the gifts of the Spirit and the authority this gives to all believers are so important to the heart of God for His Church that He is going to cause both Protestants and Catholics to pray for a new Pentecost,[1] one in which the Church will awaken afresh to the importance of the recovery of the gifts. Because without His presence and His power and His authority—apart from signs and wonders and the gifts of the Holy Spirit—many more of those who don't know Him will not be awakened to His truth. When so much has been made available to the Church, why should we settle for less? Jesus' authority to heal can be restored in this generation and for all the generations to come.

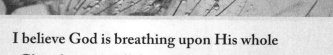

I believe God is breathing upon His whole Church, across all denominational lines, awakening all of us to His power and authority and bringing unity to the body.

While widespread ignorance of Church history has cut many believers off from our spiritual roots and made us very skeptical of the gifts of the Spirit, especially healing and miracles, that need not remain the case.

It is my belief that much of the hostility and fighting between the various camps of Christian healing springs from the deception of the enemy who comes to steal the word of God, preventing us from bringing forth a harvest of thirty, sixty, hundred fold (see Matt. 13:23; Mark 4:20). The devil has never feared our desire to get from earth to heaven, but he has great fear of us wanting to bring the power and authority of heaven to earth. The enemy of our souls works extremely hard to distract us from the reality of the good news that the Kingdom of God has come to this world in Jesus Christ. He would like to keep us focused on heaven and forgiveness in the hope that we do not notice the present reality of the availability of the power and the authority of the Kingdom here on earth. Through doctrinal strongholds, he and his demonic philosophies have been used to try and stop the fulfillment of Jesus' prayer, 'Thy Kingdom come, Thy will be done in earth, as it is in heaven'" (Matt. 6:10 KJV)."[2] But we know that the blood of the Lamb has overcome, and history clearly records that the tides are changing.

Today we must continue to wrestle against years of tradition and theology that have changed the makeup of the Church and against the traditions of those who confused the Church's understanding of itself. We must wrestle to awaken a westernized Church that has fallen asleep, so that the gospel of the Kingdom will be restored in all its fullness—a gospel of forgiveness *and* power and authority—so that our methods of evangelism are no longer limited to debate and argument but are augmented by God's gracelets of healing and working of miracles.[3]

These are exciting times for the Church. Let us press in for more, together, because Jesus intends for His *whole* Church to move in the power and authority of His Holy Spirit, in order that the Kingdom of God that was ushered in by His (Jesus') coming can be brought to bear on the kingdom of this world.

> *And with that he breathed on them and said, "Receive the Holy Spirit"* (John 20:22).

# ENDNOTES

## INTRODUCTION

1. See Matthew 4:18–22; Mark 1:14–20; Luke 5:1–11; John 1:43–50.

2. Candy Gunther Brown, "Study of the Therapeutic Effects of Proximal Intercessory Prayer (STEPP) on Auditory and Visual Impairments in Rural Mozambique," *Southern Medical Journal* 103:9 (September 2010), 864-69; Candy Gunther Brown, *Testing Prayer: Science and Healing* (Cambridge, MA: Harvard University Press, 2012).

3. See Pastor Bill Johnson's book, *The Supernatural Power of a Transformed Mind.*

4. Jesus connected the preaching of the Kingdom of God to power, as demonstrated in the gospels of Matthew and Mark and Luke—Matthew 10:7-8, 11:12, 12:28; Mark 9:1. Luke's version of the commissioning of the twelve notes both power and authority connected to the commission and says that the Kingdom of God is the same as the Kingdom of Heaven (9:11). In the book of Acts, Philip the Evangelist announces the Kingdom of God in his preaching and, as a result, there were many miraculous signs. Even a sorcerer who worked in the power of the occult was so greatly impressed by the demonstrations of power from this Kingdom that he left his sorcery and became a Christian (see Acts 8:12–19).

5.  Attendees at our meetings gave hundreds of testimonies of healing by January 2012. Global Awakening's media team recorded over 100 of these testimonies. Video testimonies may be viewed at: http://www.youtube.com/playlist?list =PLUERmgsb980UQCHzNUzFzB9qnRiZ73edZ&feature =edit_ok.

6.  I heard this emphasis in a lecture at United Theological Seminary from Jon Ruthven and Gary Greig, the two mentors I had for my doctorate program during January 2012 intensive.

## CHAPTER TWO

1.  Morton Kelsey, *Healing and Christianity* (San Francisco, CA: Harper and Row Publishers, reprinted Augsburg Fortress, 1973, 1995).

2.  Dr. John Polhill, interview by Randy Clark, Louisville, KY (1976).

3.  Wouter J. Hanegraaff, *New Age Religion and Western Culture: Esotericism in the Mirror of Secular Thought* (Albany, NY: State University of New York Press, 1988). This work provides an important understanding from a scholarly position on the New Age movement and the role of healing in the New Age movement. Also, for the role of healing in the spreading of Christianity, see Phillip Jenkins, *The Next Christendom: The Coming of Global Christianity* (New York, NY: Oxford University Press, 2002).

4.  Ramsay MacMullen, *Christianizing the Roman Empire AD 100-400* (New Haven, CT: Yale University Press, 1984), chap. 3-4. MacMullen emphasizes that the primary reason for the conversion of the Europeans from the Greco-Roman gods to Christianity was its power to deliver from demons and to heal sickness and disease. He also points out that the last god whose temples were consecrated as churches was Aesclepius, the Greco-Roman god of healing.

William DeArteaga, *Forging a Renewed Hebraic and Pauline Christianity* (Tulsa, OK: Word & Spirit Press, forthcoming). DeArteaga adds to MacMullen by pointing out how important healing was to the American Church in the final quarter of the nineteenth century and the first part of the twentieth century.

David Harrell Jr., *All Things are Possible* (Bloomington, IN: Indiana University Press, 1975). Harrell presents a scholarly portrait of the interest in healing at the mid-twentieth century. While in South Africa, a taxi cab driver shared that he had left the Pentecostal denomination to join the Zionist movement, a cult in South Africa. When asked what motivated him, he said, "I was healed through the Zionist church, so my whole family and I joined it." This is consistent with the emphasis of MacMullen. See also: Henry I. Lederle, *Theology with Spirit: The Future of the Pentecostal-Charismatic Movements in the 21st Century* (Tulsa, OK: Word & Spirit, 2010).

5.  Harvard professor of medicine, Dr. Herbert Benson, believes there could be huge tax savings to Americans through the use of self-healing practices. Herbert Benson, *Timeless Healing: The Power and Biology of Belief* (New York, NY: Simon and Schuster, 1997), 223-24.

6.  For a clear understanding of the common arguments against the promise of "greater works," review the following blog article by Dr. Michael L. Brown, entitled "The Master's Seminary Professor and John 14:12," (http://askdrbrown.org/the-masters-seminary-professor-and-john-1412/).

## CHAPTER THREE

1.  This illustrates, as emphasized by Ruthven, that faith is primarily hearing God's voice and obeying it. Jon Ruthven, *What's Wrong with Protestant Theology? Tradition vs. Biblical Emphasis* (Tulsa, OK: Word & Spirit Press, 2013), 144.

2. "Anyone who has made a careful study of the biblical subject of divine healing, having systematically treated the OT material, cannot help but feel that the floodgates of healing have opened in the pages of the NT. The trickle has become a deluge, the exceptional has become the norm, the occasional has become the commonplace, the hoped for has become the experienced, the longed for has become the realized." Michael Brown, *Israel's Divine Healer* (Grand Rapids, MI: Zondervan, 1995), 208. Brown was the author of the article, *"ropheh"* in R. Laird Harris, Gleason L. Archer, and Bruce K. Waltke, eds., *Theological Wordbook of the Old Testament* (Chicago, IL: Moody Press, 1980); see also David Green, *"rapa," Theological Dictionary of the Old Testament*, ed. G. Johannes Botterweck, Helmer Ringgren, and Heinz-Josef Fabry (Grand Rapids, MI: Eerdmans, 2004), 13:593-602.

3. See George Eldon Ladd, *The Kingdom of God* (Carlisle, PA: Paternoster Press, 1959), esp. chap. 1, 9; Brown, *Israel's Divine Healer*, 215-17, 242; Craig Keener, *Miracles: The Credibility of the New Testament Accounts* (Grand Rapids, MI: Baker Academic, 2011), 1:11, 1:24, 1:61, 1:66, 1:76, 1:96, 1:262, 1:389, 1:484, 1:506-519, 1:511, 2:606, 2:736, 2:767, 2:785; Jon Ruthven, *On the Cessation of the Charismata: The Protestant Polemic on Postbiblical Miracles* (Tulsa, OK: Word & Spirit Press, 2011), 97-107, 175-77; J.P. Moreland, *Kingdom Triangle: Recover the Christian Mind, Renovate the Soul, Restore the Spirit's Power* (Grand Rapids, MI: Zondervan, 2007), 135, 168-74, 177.

For ramifications of Kingdom theology to healing see Paul King, *Only Believe: Examining the Origin and Development of Classic and Contemporary "Word of Faith" Theologies* (Tulsa, OK: Word & Spirit, 2008), 73, 95, 98, 133, 134; Ken Blue, *Authority to Heal* (Downers Grove, IL: InterVarsity Press, 1987), 2:79-89; John Wimber, *Power Healing* (San Francisco, CA: Harper and Row, 1987), 157-59; Alexander Venter, *Doing Healing: How to Minister God's Kingdom in the Power of the Spirit* (Cape Town, South Africa: Vineyard International, 2009), 66-98, 125-36.

4.  Though all are commissioned, this does not mean that all will experience the same *degree* of frequency or magnitude of the gifts of healing and miracles in their lives. For example, those doing missionary work in other cultures among other faiths often see more healings and miracles than those in a Christian culture, but this is also dependent upon the missionaries not being cessationist. First Corinthians 12:28 indicates that there are varying degrees of giftedness in the New Testament. To paraphrase the language of Wimber, "all should expect the gifts of the Spirit for healing to occur situationally, but not all have a constituted gift of healing." This does not negate the basic premise that all are commissioned to heal and cast out demons.

5.  Howe, *Anointed by the Spirit*, (Mary Lake, FL; Charisma House, 2012), 10, Kindle Ed.

6.  Brown, *Israel's Divine Healer*, 29, 165.

7.  View video testimony here: https://www.youtube.com/watch?v=G8sB7t2qbUw.

## CHAPTER FOUR

1.  These are the three most common periods used for the termination of the "sign" gifts. There is disagreement among cessationists about when the gifts ended. Related to this passage is the largely overlooked general statement: "God empowers all [Greek: *charismata*] in all" (see 1 Cor. 12:7).

2.  Jon Ruthven, e-mail message to me, April 3, 2013.

3.  Jack Deere, *Surprised by the Power of the Spirit: Discovering How God Speaks and Heals Today* (Grand Rapids, MI: Zondervan, 1996); 253-66.

4.  Schlier, *Theological Dictionary of the New Testament (TDNT)*, ed. Gerhard Kittel and Gerhard Friedrich, trans. Geoffrey W.

Bromiley (Grand Rapids, MI: Eerdmans, 1977), s.v., "*bebaioō*," 1:600-603.

5.  Gary Shogren, "How Did They Suppose 'The Perfect' Would Come? 1 Corinthians 13:8-12 in Patristic Exegesis" in *Journal of Pentecostal Theology* 15 (1999): 99-121; Gary Shogren, "Christian Prophecy and Canon in the Second Century: A Response to B.B. Warfield," *Journal of the Evangelical Theological Society* 40, no.4 (December 1977): 609-626; Gary Shogren, "First Corinthians: An Exegetical-Pastoral Commentary," http://openoureyeslord.files.wordpress.com/2012/05/shogren_1_corinthians.pdf (accessed April 29, 2013); Anthony C Thiselton, *The Holy Spirit: In Biblical Teaching, Through the Centuries, and Today* (Grand Rapids, MI: Eerdmans, 2013); Anthony C. Thiselton, *First Corinthians*, 3182-3281, Kindle ebook.

    In Thiselton's larger commentary, *First Epistle*, he discusses in greater depth the issue of cessationist views of tongues, 1061-64; Gordon D. Fee, *The First Epistle to the Corinthians: The New International Commentary on the New Testament* (Grand Rapids, MI: Eerdmans, 1987); I. Howard Marshall, *New Testament Theology: Many Witnesses, One Gospel* (Downers Grove, IL: Inter Varsity Press, 2004), 3, Kindle ebook.

6.  There seems to be a parallel to Moses' statement in Exodus 33:13, "If you are pleased with me, teach me your ways so I may know you and continue to find favor with you."

7.  Randy Clark, "Healing and the Glory of God," in *Empowered: A School of Healing and Impartation Workbook*, ed. Randy Clark (Mechanicsburg, PA: Global Awakening, 2012), 191-201. A study of the word *glory* in the Hebrew and the Greek shows that the main way God glorifies His name is through signs and wonders, miracles and healings. This correlation of glory and miracle was higher than any other category (see Clark, *Empowered*, 192-94). The second highest dealt with the pillar of fire by night and the cloud by day of the Exodus wanderings. Nothing else came close.

8.  "I am writing these things to you about those who are trying to lead you astray. As for you, the anointing you received from him remains in you, and you do not need anyone to teach you. But as his anointing teaches you about all things and as that anointing is real, not counterfeit—just as it has taught you, remain in him" (1 John 2:26–28).

## CHAPTER FIVE

1.  See Timothy Berry, Annie Byrne, Chris Ishak, and Randy Clark, *Entertaining Angels: Engaging the Unseen Realm* (Mechanicsburg, PA: Apostolic Network of Global Awakening, 2008), 14-16.

2.  The following is an excerpt from The Creed of Chalcedon dated A.D. 451, "We, then, following the holy Fathers, all with one consent, teach people to confess one and the same Son, our Lord Jesus Christ, the same perfect in Godhead and also perfect in manhood; truly God and truly man, of a reasonable [rational] soul and body; consubstantial [co-essential] with the Father according to the Godhead, and consubstantial with us according to the Manhood; in all things like unto us, without sin." Christian Apologetics and Research Ministry, "Chalcedonian Creed, (A.D. 451)," http://carm.org/christianity/creeds-and-confessions/chalcedonian-creed-451-ad (accessed July 13, 2013).

3.  Moreland states, "When I was saved in the late 1960s, I was taught that Jesus' miracles proved He was God because He did them from His divine nature. It has become clear to me, however, that this was wrong, for Jesus' public ministry was done as He, a perfect man, did what He saw His Father doing in dependence on the filling of the Holy Spirit." Moreland, *Kingdom Triangle*, 174-175.

    Oden notes: "As a man, Jesus walked day by day in radical dependence upon God the Spirit, prayed, and spoke by the power of the Spirit. In portraying Jesus as constantly dependent upon the Spirit, the Gospels were not challenging or questioning his deity or divine Sonship. Rather, as eternal Son the theandric person already was truly God, while as a man, Jesus was truly human, bone of our bone, flesh of our flesh, seed of Abraham, whose humanity was continually replenished by the Spirit (Luke 4:14; Heb. 2:14-17). He did not walk or speak by his own independent human power, but by power of the Spirit. Every gift requisite to the Son's mission was provided by the Spirit. The implications of this understanding of Jesus' ministry are remarkable: 'Jesus is living proof of how those who are his followers may exceed the limitations of their humanness in order that they, like him, might carry to completion against all odds their God-given mission in life—by the Holy Spirit.' It is becoming clear that when Jesus said that 'greater works than these he [i.e., the one who believes in Jesus] will do, because I go to the Father' (John 14:12), he meant it in the ordinary way these words would be interpreted." Thomas C. Oden, *Systematic Theology* (San Francisco, CA: Harper, 1992), 3:347n17. See also: Gerald Hawthorne, *The Presence and the Power: The Significance of the Holy Spirit in the Life and Ministry of Jesus* (Dallas, TX: Word, 1991), 234.

4.     The Bible does not say how long Paul had this illness; just that he had an illness. This was not what Paul was referencing in Second Corinthians regarding his thorn in the flesh; instead, this verse refers either to people or evil spirits, due to the fact that the only OT verses dealing with a thorn in the flesh refer to a personality, not a sickness. The three OT passages dealing with a thorn are Numbers 33:55; Joshua 23:13; Ezekiel 28:24.

# CHAPTER SIX

1.     Revival in Mozambique, led by Rolland and Heidi Baker, has seen roughly 10,000 churches started and over 1,000,000 new believers come into the Kingdom of God and was

birthed through a prophetic word and a powerful impartation of the Holy Spirit. Likewise, the ministry of Norwegian pastor Leif Hetland has brought 1,000,000 Muslims into the Kingdom of God and began with a prophetic word and an impartation. Pastor Henry Madava in the Ukraine is another example. As a result of a powerful time of impartation, his ministry has seen over 1,000,000 people born again. The list continues with powerful impartations to pastors in the former Soviet Union (Catch the Fire Moscow 1995), in Russia (Oleg Serov and Shasha), and in Brazil, where in four years alone (1999–2004) there have been approximately 100,000 healings when Randy and Global Awakening teams prayed for the sick. Brazil has also seen thousands born again as a result of impartation to pastors and leaders, such as Marcelo Cassagrande. In Argentina the healing ministry of Marcelo Diaz was birthed in the oldest Baptist church in the nation when I (Randy) laid hands on him.

2. Gordon Fee, *The First Epistle to the Corinthians: The New International Commentary on the New Testament* (Grand Rapids, MI: William. B. Eerdmans Publishing Company, 1993).

3. Ruthven, *On the Cessation*, 195-202; Greig and Springer, *The Kingdom and the Power*.

4. Acts 9:17-18: "Then Ananias went to the house and entered it. Placing his hands on Saul, he said, 'Brother Saul, the Lord—Jesus, who appeared to you on the road as you were coming here—has sent me so that you may see again and be filled with the Holy Spirit.' Immediately, something like scales fell from Saul's eyes, and he could see again. He got up and was baptized." (Ananias was not an apostle.)

5. For example, see the Assemblies of God position papers, http://www.ag.org/top/beliefs/position_papers/pp_downloads/pp_endtime_revival.pdf.

6. A powerful example that debunks this thinking is the story of Dan Bohi found in the Conclusion of this book.

# CHAPTER SEVEN

1.  The following translations use "faith in God": New International Version, Holman Christian Standard Bible, King James Version, New American Bible, La Biblia de las Americas, New American Standard Bible 1995 (however, the interlinear of this version uses *have faith God*), New American Standard Bible 1977, Authorized Standard Version, Nouvelle Edition de Geneve 1979 (French), Nueva Riveduta 1994 (Italian), Reina Valera 1909 (Spanish), Schlater 1951 (German), World English Bible, Today's New International Version, The Darby Translation Bible, Weymouth New Testament Bible, New International Reader's Version, The Webster Bible, English Standard Version, Mounce, The Net Bible, and The Bishop's Bible. The following translations translate Εχετε πιστιν θεου to *have faith of God*, Douay-Rheims, Geneva 1599, Young's Literal Translation, and the Bible in Basic English 1965.

2.  Understanding the Greek phrase *pistin theou* as "the faith of God," that is, as a subjective genitive of *theos* "God"—as rendered by both the second century A.D. Greek text of Tatian's Diatessaron § 33 ("Let there be in you the faith of God") and the fifth-century Syriac Peshitta ("You should have faith of God"). For the Syriac Peshitta translation, see Janet M. Magiera, *Aramaic Peshitta New Testament Translation* (Truth or Consequences, NM: Light of the Word Ministry, 2006), 129. For the Diatessaron translation, see E.C. Richardson and B. Pick, *The Ante-Nicene Fathers* (New York, NY: Scribners, 1903), 9:94.

    Charles Wesley understood Mark 11:22 this way: "I want the true divinity, the faith of God, the power in me." S.T. Kimbrough, *Orthodox and Wesleyan Scriptural Understanding and Practice* (Crestwood, NY: St. Vladimir's Seminary Press, 2005), 179. The subjective genitive interpretation is in contrast to the equally possible objective genitive interpretation of *pistin theou*, "faith in God." For the subjective genitive interpretation of similar occurrences of genitive nouns or pronouns referring to God or Christ following *pistis* "faith" in Pauline epistles ("the faith/faithfulness of God/Christ"), see R.N. Longenecker, *Paul, Apostle of Liberty* (New York, NY: Harper & Row, 1964), 149-52; G. Howard, "The Faith of Christ," *Expository Times* 85 (1974), 212-15; S.K. Williams, "Again *Pistis Christou*," *Catholic Biblical Quarterly* 49 (1987), 431-47; R.B. Hays, "The Faith of Jesus Christ: An Investigation of the Narrative Substructure of Galatians 3:1-4:11," in *Society of Biblical Literature Dissertation Series* 56 (Chico, CA: Scholars, 1983).

3.     Zeno Vendler, *Linguistics in Philosophy* (Ithaca, NY: Cornell University, 1967), 106, 115.

4.     Bauer and Gingrich, 420-21; meaning number 3: "to take a hold on something...grip...seize."

5.     See reference referring to Acts 3:16 ("the faith that comes through him [Christ]"), David Peterson comments, "Jesus himself is the source and inspiration for the faith that secures God's blessing." David Peterson, *The Acts of the Apostles* (Grand Rapids, MI: Eerdmans, 2009), 177.

6.     The whole issue related to stative is based on insights from Dr. Gary Greig.

7.     Catholic, Orthodox, Arminian/Wesleyan, and Calvinist systems of theology embrace the truth regarding prevenient grace. For the Catholic, Orthodox, and Arminian/Wesleyan, this grace that enables one to believe in the gospel is resistible, while in Calvinism it is not.

8.     *The Book of Discipline of The United Methodist Church 2004* (Nashville, TN: United Methodist Publishing, 2004), section 1.

9.     Jacobus Armnius and Petrus Bertius, *The Works of James Arminius, D.D., Formerly Professor of Divinity in the University of Leyden* (Auburn, NY: Derby and Miller, 1853), 4:472.

10. Charles S. Price, *The Real Faith for Healing*, ed. Harold J. Chadwick (North Brunswick, NJ: Bridge-Logos, 1997), 24-58.

11. Howe, *Anointed by the Spirit*, 58, Kindle Ed.

12. This insight regarding the relationship between faith for miracles and revelation is based upon a conversation with Omar Cabrera in Omar's home in Buenos Aires, Argentina in 1996. On this trip nine hours were given to interviewing Omar Cabrera, Carlos Annacondia, Dr. Pablo Deiros, Dr. Carlos Mrarida (both co-pastors of the oldest and second largest Baptist church in Argentina), Gereimo Preim, Claudio Freidzon, and Victor Lorenzo, all key leaders of the Argentine revival. See Randy Clark, *Lighting Fires* (Mechanicsburg, PA: Global Awakening, 1998), 121-22.

13. Owen Jorgensen, *Supernatural: The Life of William Branham*, vol. 3, *The Man and His Commission* (Tucson, AZ: Tucson Tabernacle, 1994), 136, 159-60.

14. I have also had the privilege of working with and dialoguing with more than ten ministers who are noted for their ministry of healing, including Heidi Baker, Bill Johnson, James Maloney, Omar Cabrera, Carlos Annacondia, Leif Hetland, Henry Madava, Cal Pierce, Ian Andrews, Jim and Ramona Rickard, and Todd White.

15. Jesus also refers to little faith in Matthew 6:30; 8:26; 14:31; 16:8; 17:20; Luke 12:28. He refers to great faith in Matthew 8:10; 15:28; Luke 7:9; John 14:12.

16. "When the word grace is used in the New Testament, there is the suggestion of God's presence. Therefore grace could be defined as 'God's empowering presence,' and as such it includes all that is meant by the word 'power,' that is, both divine authority and dynamic power." Jim B. McClure, *Grace Revisited* (Geelong, Australia: Trailblazer Books, 2010), 61.

17. Wimber, *Power Healing*, 148-51.

18. Bultmann, *TDNT*, s.v. *"pistis,"* 6:174-82. It is interesting not only in considering what Bultmann covers in his article on faith, but also to note what he does not mention or develop. He offers no discussion of the relationship between faith and healing, faith and miracles, faith and signs and wonders, faith and power. For this discussion, see Ruthven, *What's Wrong*, 127-59.

19. Ruthven, *What's Wrong*; Ruthven, *On the Cessation*; Greig and Springer, *The Kingdom and the Power*; 149-61.

20. Ruthven, *What's Wrong*, esp. chap. 7–10.

21. Bill Johnson and Randy Clark, *The Essential Guide to Healing*; Randy Clark, *Words of Knowledge* (Mechanicsburg, PA: Global Awakening), 2011.

22. Debrunner, *TDNT*, s.v. *"logos,"* 4:69-77.

23. John 14–16, esp. 14:15–21; 15:1–8; 16:12–15.

24. For more dialogue on how faith comes to a person, one should watch the ten video interviews, each two hours in length, that were conducted with key leaders in the ministry of healing today. Those interviewed were Bill Johnson, overseer of the Global Legacy network and senior leader of Bethel Church; Heidi Baker, co-leader of Iris Ministries in Mozambique; Jim and Ramona Rickard, overseers of the International Association of Healing Ministries; Leif Hetland, overseer of the Global Awareness Ministry and Network; Cal Pierce, overseer of the International Healing Rooms; Henry Madava, senior leader of Victory Christian Church Network and founder of the international ministry Christ for All Cities in Kiev, Ukraine; James Maloney, president of the ACTS Group International; Todd White, a powerful evangelist who moves in prophetic evangelism and healing evangelism; Ian Andrews, apostolic director of the International Association of Healing Ministries and founder of Citadel Ministries; and myself, overseer of the Apostolic Network of Global Awakening and the ministry of Global Awakening. These testimonies are available in the first physical healing course in

the *Christian Healing Certification Program.* The book *Healing Unplugged,* by Bill Johnson and Randy Clark, (Grand Rapids, MI: Chosen Books Publishing, 2012) is the transcription of about four and a half hours of interviews between Bill Johnson and myself.

Each of these ten interviewees answered the same five questions: 1) the story of how they were called and major events or experiences; 2) how they grew and developed further in the area of healing and miracles; 3) what were the break-through events in their lives that caused them to see more healings and miracles; 4) how they developed the ability to see and/or hear the Holy Spirit's leading; 5) what were the four or five most miraculous healings and/or deliverances they experienced. Watching or reading these testimonies gives one a greater appreciation for faith as a grace and how the grace gifts help to build faith.

## CHAPTER EIGHT

1.  The night after defending my doctorate research, at Living Word Church in Dayton, Ohio eight out of twelve with implanted materials reported healing for a total of 66 percent healed. At the following year's Voice of the Apostles conference there were scores healed of complications following surgeries involving implanted materials with the percentage healed being 68 percent.

2.  The man who testified he had an implanted metal rod in his right arm shared during the meeting that he also had seventeen screws in that arm. Video testimony may be viewed here: http://www.youtube.com/watch?v=BXM58ji -5kI&feature=youtu.be.

3.  This was the most ever in the United States up to that time. Since then, as mentioned in an earlier footnote, there has been a greater percentage, which involved a larger group involving

scores of people—the meeting in Dayton, Ohio and the Voice of the Apostles conference in August 2013.

4.  See Matthew 4:23; 9:35; 11:5; Luke 9:6; Acts 8:4–8; 10:36; 14:8–18; 16:17; Romans 15:14–20; 2 Corinthians 12:12; Galatians 3:5.

5.  This language, "not a problem to be achieved, but a promise to be received," I gained from Leif Hetland, a powerful apostolic evangelist among the Muslims of Pakistan, who has led over one million Muslims to Jesus. He has been a regular part of many of Global Awakening's Schools of Healing and Impartation. He began working with Global Awakening in 2004 and has repeatedly used this language in every school.

6.  Clark, *Empowered*, 191-204.

# CHAPTER NINE

1.  Randy Clark, and Susan Thompson. *Healing Energy: Whose Energy Is It?* (Mechanicsburg, PA: Global Awakening, 2013), 32.

2.  The wonderful *Narrative, or, a Faithful Account of the French Prophets, their Agitations, Extasies, and Inspirations* (Boston, 1742), Appendix, 97-104. This was formerly attributed to Charles Chauncy but recently questioned. The following is from Lovejoy, *Religious Enthusiasm in the Great Awakening*, 62-63, as told to me by Charity Cook, staff member at Global Awakening: "It is a *strong presumption* therefore against any, that they have a *strange Fire* working in them, when they are seized with *swoonings*, and have bodily Representations of those Things, which are *spiritually* to be discerned, because these *Sights* have been common among *Enthusiasts* of all Sorts, but seldom or never among *solid* Christians. In the Beginning of the Reformation, there were Swarms of those, who pretended to these *extraordinary* Matters; but they were always esteemed a Clog to the Reformation, and a disgrace of it: Nor are *visions* and *trances* more common anywhere, than among

*Papists*; The lives of their Saints...are filled with Relations in this Kind."

3. Gnosticism was a second-century heretical movement prevalent within the Church, consisting of diverse beliefs and based on "secret knowledge." For further insight along this line, Edward William Fudge, *The Fire that Consumes: A Biblical and Historical Study of the Doctrine of Final Punishment* (Lincoln, NE: Verdict, 2001); Anthony C. Thiselston, *Life after Death: A New Approach to the Last Things* (Grand Rapids, MI: Eerdmans, 2011); Edward William Fudge and Robert A. Peterson, *Two Views of Hell: A Biblical and Theological Dialogue* (Downers Grove, IL: InterVarsity Press, 2000).

4. Justin Martyr, *The Second Apology of Justin Martyr for the Christians* (Rome: c. 161), www.earlychristianwritings.com/text/justinmartyr-secondapology.html (accessed September 24, 2011).

5. Tertullian. "To Scapula," (Carthage: c. 217), www.earlychristianwritings.com/text/tertullian05.html (accessed September 24, 2011).

6. Tertullian was one of the three greatest theologians of the first 1,200 years of the Church along with Augustine and Aquinas. However, later in his life he joined the unorthodox Montanists. The above quote was from his orthodox period of ministry.

7. George Montague and Killian McDonnell, *Christian Initiation and Baptism in the Holy Spirit: Evidence from the First Eight Centuries* (Collegeville, MN: Liturgical, 1994), 108. Again, the above quote was from his orthodox period of ministry.

8. Origen, *Contra Celsus* (Alexandria: c. 248), www.earlychristianwritings.com/text/origen161.html (accessed September 24, 2011).

9. Irenaeus, *Against Heresies* (Gaul, c. 180), www.columbia.edu/cu/augustine/arch/irenaeus (accessed September 24, 2011).

10. Ted Olbrich, interview with me, Cambodia Church Planting and the Need for Greater Power Evangelism, Albuquerque, NM (June 22, 2012). I recently had Ted come and speak at the 2015 Voice of the Apostles. He told me that the churches had grown from 3,000 to 6,000 in the two years since we went and had special meetings for his top leaders, about 400 of them. The purpose of the meeting was for impartation with the laying on of hands. As a result of what God did to these leaders there was 100 percent growth of churches in two years.

11. Kelsey, *Healing and Christianity*, 120.

12. Ibid.

13. Ibid., 107, 121.

14. Clark, School of Healing and Impartation: Empowered Workbook (Mechanicsburg, PA: Global Awakening, 2012), 58; Kelsey, *Healing and Christianity*, 159.

15. Kelsey, *Healing and Christianity*, 133.

16. Clark, School of Healing and Impartation: Empowered Workbook (Mechanicsburg, PA: Global Awakening, 2012), 58; Kelsey, *Healing and Christianity*, 159.

17. Kelsey, *Healing and Christianity*, 167.

18. St. Augustine, *The City of God*, (New York: Fathers of the Church, 1954), 445.

19. Ibid.

20. Gregory Boyd, *God at War: The Bible and Spiritual Conflict* (Downers Grove, IL: InterVarsity Press, 1997).

21. Clark, *Empowered*, 59-60; F. van der Meer, *Augustine the Bishop: The Life and Work of a Father of the Church*, (London: Sheen & Ward, 1961), 549-53.

22. Elizabeth A. Livingstone, *Studia Patristica, Papers Presented to the Tenth International Conference on Patristic Studies* (Leuven, Belgium: Peeters Press, 1989), 22:189. This quote is paraphrased by Livingstone from the Latin.

# CHAPTER TEN

1. Morton Kelsey has written about this influence in his book, *Healing and Christianity*. However, when writing my thesis I was informed by a leading Roman Catholic theologian that Kelsey had misunderstood Aquinas and that Aquinas was very open to the supernatural and the gifts of the Holy Spirit. I believe Dr. Mary Healey is correct and Dr. Kelsey has misunderstood Aquinas. However, I do believe there was an eventual influence from rationalism associated with Aristotelian philosophy that created less room for the supernatural in the Church. In this way it is true that Luther and Calvin, along with the other major reformers, did not challenge the sixteenth-century understanding of the faith, which was much less open to the supernatural than the earlier periods of the Church.

2. Henry Worsley, *The Life of Martin Luther in Two Volumes* (London: Bell and Daldy, 1856), 286-88. Emphasis added.

3. Theodore J. Tappert, *Luther: Letters of Spiritual Counsel* (Vancouver, BC: Regent College Publishing, 1960, republished 2003), 48-49.

4. Th. Jungkunz, "Charismatic Renewal," *Concordia Theological Monthly* 42:1 (1971), 5-23.

5. Thomas Boys, *The Suppressed Evidenced: Or Proofs of the Miraculous Faith and Experience of the Church of Jesus Christ In All Ages*, 1832. Google Books, http://books.google .com/books?id=JkopAAAAYAAJ&printsec=frontcover &source=gbs_ge_summary_r&cad=0#v=onepage&q&f=false (accessed March 5, 2012).

6. John Wimber shared this with a group comprised of two groups, one from Colorado, and another that I led from Illinois. This was at a healing meeting in Houston in 1984.

7. George Fox, *George Fox's Book of Miracles* (Philadelphia, PA: Friends General Conference and Quaker Home Service, 2000).

8.  Paul Chappell, "Healing Movements," *Dictionary of Pentecostal and Charismatic Movements*, edited by Stanley M. Burgess and Gary B. McGee (Grand Rapids, MI: Zondervan Publishing House, 1996), 354.

9.  Ibid., 355.

10. Friedrich Zündel, *The Awakening: One Man's Battle with Darkness* (Farmington, PA: Plough, 1999), passim. Chappell, "Healing Movements," 355.

11. Chappell, "Healing Movements," 355.

12. Ibid., 356.

13. Ibid.

14. Ibid., 357; Joe. McIntyre, *E.W. Kenyon and His Message of Faith* (Bothell, WA: Empowering Grace, 2010), 76-80; King, *Only Believe*, 105-108.

15. Ibid.

16. Chappell, "Healing Movements," 358; McIntyre, *E.W. Kenyon*, 76-80; King, *Only Believe*, 105-108.

17. Chappell, "Healing Movements," 358-59.

18. Ibid., 359-63.

19. Ibid. 363.

20. McIntyre, *E.W. Kenyon*, 77-78.

21. Ruthven, *On the Cessation*, 7; Chappell, "Healing Movements," 363.

22. Chappell, "Healing Movements," 363.

23. Based upon a discussion with prophetic itinerate minister James Goll who had gone to Zion and visited Dowie's home, 2011.

24. "Healing and Revival," *Healing and Revival Press*, 2004, http://healingandrevival.com/BioCSPrice.htm (accessed April 15, 2012).

25. F.F. Bosworth, *Christ the Healer* (Old Tappan, NJ: Fleming H. Revell Co., 1973), 14-39.

26. Price, *The Real Faith*, 46.

27. Roberts Lairdon, *John G. Lake* (Tulsa, OK: Albury Publishing, 1999).

28. David Harrell, Jr., *All Things Are Possible* (Bloomington, IN: Indiana University Press, 1975).

29. Kathryn Kuhlman, *I Believe in Miracles* (Alachua, FL: Bridge-Logos, 1962, 1990). I was nineteen when I read this book. I was enthralled by it, reading it in one setting. I was in tears and another seed was planted in my heart to desire a breakthrough to see healing in my ministry.

30. King, *Only Believe*, 200, 214, 153. King provides a fair and honest treatment of these men in light of their critics.

31. Chappell, "Healing Movements," 353-74, esp. 374. However, both Joe McIntyre and Paul King have refuted this view of Chappell in their writings.

32. Chappell, "Healing Movements" 353-74. McIntyre, *E.W. Kenyon*, 61. King, *Only Believe*, 293.

33. Dave Hunt and T.A. McMahon, *Seduction of Christianity* (Eugene, OR: Harvest House Publishers, 1985).

34. Dave Hunt, *Beyond Seduction: A Return to Biblical Christianity* (Eugene, OR: Harvest House Publishers, 1987).

35. D.R. McConnell, *A Different Gospel: Biblical and Historical Insights into the Word of Faith Movement* (Peabody, MA: Hendrickson Publishers, 1995).

36. John MacArthur, *Charismatic Chaos* (Grand Rapids, MI: Zondervan, 1992).

37. Hank Hanegraaff, *Christianity in Crisis* (Eugene, OR: Harvest House Publishers, 1993).

38. King, *Only Believe*, 64-65, 144, 154, especially 161, 227, 229, 245, 301, 368.

39. McIntyre, *E.W. Kenyon*, 36-37.

# CHAPTER ELEVEN

1. Clark and Thompson, *Healing Energy*, 29-30.

2. Ramsay MacMullen, *Christianizing the Roman Empire AD 100-400* (New Haven, CT: Yale University Press, 1984), 55-58.

3. See Paul Tournier, *The Meaning of Persons* (New York, NY: Harper and Row, 1965).

4. This begins to change with the field of psychosomatic medicine that is rediscovering and affirming (though often unaware) the biblical view of a person as a whole and that if one part becomes ill it can affect the other two. This school of medicine is also discovering the spiritual aspects of disease (i.e., the soul as the seat of will and emotions). Souls become sick when the principles of Scripture are not followed. For example, the following emotions are seen in the biblical accounts as dangerous and to be avoided in one's life: unforgiveness, anger, bitterness, and a cynical and judgmental attitude. The following works reveal this biblical understanding of the person as a whole: Tournier, *The Meaning of Persons*; Rene Pelleya-Kouri, *Praying Doctors: Jesus in the Office—Testimony and Basic Training Manual* (Bloomington, IN: Trafford, 2009); Phil Mason, *Quantum Glory: The Science of Heaven Invading Earth* (Chang Mai: Acts Co, 2010); Jeff Levin, *God, Faith and Health: Exploring the Spirituality-Healing Connection* (New York, NY: John Wiley, 2001); Harold G. Koenig, *The Healing Power of Faith: How Belief and Prayer Can Help You Triumph Over Disease* (New York, NY: Simon and Schuster, 2001); Harold G. Koenig and Harvey J. Cohen, eds., *The Link between Religion and Health: Psychoneuroimmunology and the Faith Factor* (New York, NY: Oxford University Press, 2002); Harold G. Koenig, *The Healing Connection: The Story of a Physician's Search for the Link Between Faith and Health* (Philadelphia, PA: Templeton, 2000); Kenneth Winston Caine, Brian Paul Kaufman,

and Bernie S. Siegel, *Prayer, Faith, and Healing: Cure Your Body, Heal Your Mind and Restore Your Soul* (Kutztown, PA: Rodale, 1999); James P. Gills, *God's Prescription for Healing: Five Divine Gifts of Healing* (Lake Mary, FL: Siloam, 2004); E.L. House, *The Psychology of Orthodoxy* (New York, NY: Fleming H. Revell, 1913); Harold G. Koenig, Michael E. McCullough, and David B. Larson, *Handbook of Religion and Health* (New York, NY: Oxford University Press, 2001, Revell, 1913); Frederic Flach, *Faith, Healing, and Miracles* (New York, NY: Hatherleigh, 2000); Michael Foust, "Pew: Christianity has Become Global Faith in Past Century," *Baptist Press: News with a Christian Perspective* (Nashville, TN: Southern Baptist Convention, December 21, 2011).

5.  Randy Clark and Martha Wertz, *Out of Darkness Into the Light: The Story of One Woman's Journey into the New Age and How God set Her Free,* forthcoming 2017.

6.  Reiki is an energy healing modality designed and rooted in an ancient demon-worshiping religion that is a form of Tibetan occultism. For a more in-depth look at Reiki and other New Age energy healing modalities see Clark and Thompson, *Healing Energy.*

# CHAPTER TWELVE

1.  Rudolph Bultmann was one of the earlier exponents of the higher critical method of Bible interpretation, and there were other theologians who have accepted historiography that is based upon Enlightenment rationalism, including all of the theologians involved in the Jesus Seminar. Bultmann said, "Man's knowledge and mastery of the world have advanced to such an extent through science and technology that it is no longer possible for anyone seriously to hold to the New Testament view of the world—in fact there is no one who does…. Now that the forces and laws of nature have been discovered, we can no longer believe in spirits, whether good

or evil." Rudolph Bultmann, et al., *Kerygma and Myth, A Theological Debate*, ed. Hans Werner Bartsch, trans. Reginald H. Fuller (New York, NY: Harper Touch, 1961), 4.

C.H. Dodd said, "Jesus, as he is represented, shared the views of his contemporaries regarding the authorship of books of the Old Testament, or the phenomena of 'demon possession'—which views we could not accept without violence to our sense of truth." C.H. Dodd, *The Authority of the Bible* (New York, NY: HarperCollins, 1958), 237. Another example of the effect of the historical-critical method is its view of the Bible as the word of God. C.H. Dodd said, "Not God but Paul is the author of the epistle to the Romans." In regard to the apostles or the prophets hearing the word of God spoken to them, Dodd believed they were really having a "hallucination under trance conditions"; another interpretation of their experience was "the creative imagination of the poet at work." Dodd, *The Authority of the Bible*, 16, 81.

Heinrich Vogel states, "The early criticism was directed mainly to pointing out the things in the Bible that modern man could no longer believe. This was the rationalism against which orthodox Lutherans protested so loudly. This scholarly unbelief parading in the sheep's clothing of Christian learning did much to undermine faith in the divine character of the Bible, and men began to study the Bible as they would any other book." Heinrich J. Vogel, "Pernicious Presuppositions of the Historical-Critical Method of Bible Interpretation," *Essay File Wisconsin Lutheran Seminary Library*, 3 (June 1974), http://www.wlsessays.net/node/1187 (accessed April 29, 2013), especially the section, "Types of Criticism."

See also Siegbert W. Becker, "The Historical-Critical Method of Bible Interpretation," http://www.wlsessays.net/files/BeckerHistorical.pdf (accessed April 29, 2013). In section two, "How Does the Historical-Critical Method Affect the Church Today," Becker states, "The one thing that stands out in all various forms of historical criticism, whether it is source criticism, form criticism, redaction criticism, tradition criticism, or *Sachkritik,* is always this that the method sets the learned scholar above the Scriptures in the position of judge. Whether this is admitted or not it is always and invariably true. And, this is no accidental part of the process, but rather it is built into the method as part, if not the whole, of its essence. Without the assumption that the human scholar is able and authorized to determine what is historical and factual in the Bible and what is not, there simply could not be a historical-critical method of Bible interpretation."

Walter Wink had stinging words regarding historical biblical criticism. He said, "Historical biblical criticism is bankrupt.... It is bankrupt solely because it is incapable of achieving what most of its practitioners considered its purpose to be: so to interpret Scriptures that the past becomes alive and illumines our present with new possibilities of human and social transformation." Walter Wink, *The Bible in Human Transformation* (Minneapolis, MN: Augsburg Fortress, 2010), 1.

2. This was taught in New Testament classes at the Southern Baptist Theological Seminary; however, Dr. Dale Moody believed in the earlier dates. I attended the Southern Baptist Theological Seminary from 1974 to 1977.

   For the same reason, most of my teachers in the religious studies classes in college and later in seminary would not believe Daniel wrote Daniel, but someone else wrote it after 167 B.C. because the book of Daniel has too accurate a description of what Antiochius Ephiphanes did to the temple of Jerusalem in 167 B.C.

3. This was what was taught at the Southern Baptist Theological Seminary in the course "Apocalyptic Literature," which included Daniel. It should be noted that the seminary went through a major shift from liberalism to conservative scholarship beginning in 1978. However, this scholarship shift was to a strong cessationist position. The result would

be neither graduates under the liberal years or the Calvinistic years would have an expectation of healing today.

4. Ruthven, *What's Wrong*, 10-12.

5. The problem with this position is that the primary purpose of miracles was not to give evidence of correct doctrine, but instead they were part of the gospel, the good news that the Kingdom of God was at hand, that in Jesus' ministry the Kingdom had been inaugurated and would continue until it was consummated in His second coming.

6. Ruthven, *On the Cessation*, 169-86, esp. 172, 176.

7. Craig Keener points out that Barth "highly respected Blumhardt, who had a healing and exorcism ministry a generation or two earlier." Craig Keener, e-mail message to author, March 26, 2013. The strength of Barth's commitment to cessationism needs further study.

8. DeArteaga, *Forging a Renewed Hebraic and Pauline Christianity*, 66-71.

9. Joseph R. Hoffman, "Skeptifying Belief by Van Harvey," *The New Oxonian: Religion and Culture for the Intellectually Impatient*, http://rjosephhoffmann.wordpress.com/2011/03/09/the-historian-and-the-believer-by-van-harvey (accessed May 4, 2012).

10. B.B. Warfield, *Counterfeit Miracles* (New York, NY: Charles Scribner's Sons, 1918).

11. The State of Tennessee v. John Thomas Scopes was a very public battle between Fundamentalists and Modernists with modernists gaining the upper hand resulting in Darwin's theory of evolution being taught in U.S. public schools.

12. William E. Hordern, "Fundamentalism and Conservative Christianity: The Defense of Orthodoxy," in *A Layman's Guide to Protestant Theology* (New York, NY: Macmillan, 1974), 51-72.

13. This would lead to the demise of many mainline denominations, especially the United Methodists. This

anti-supernaturalism is one of the reasons why the Methodist Episcopal Church lost so many members to the new Holiness denominations that split out primarily from the Methodist denomination.

14. William L. DeArteaga, *Quenching the Spirit: Examining Centuries of Opposition to the Moving of the Holy Spirit* (Lake Mary, FL: Creation House, 1992), 116-29; DeArteaga, *Forging*, 254-60, forthcoming. This does not mean there were no Methodists who continued to believe in healing or practiced praying for the sick. They were, however, a small minority within the denomination.

15. During the mid-nineties and even now, Hank Hanegraaff, the "Bible Answer Man" who has been on over 450 conservative Christian radio stations, has played a similar role to the Reformed B.B. Warfield and the Methodist James Buckley of an earlier generation of critics. Yet he claims to be a Charismatic, not a cessationist. However, he argues like a cessationist, and he often has used the sentence, "Healing is possible, but it is not normative." Hanegraaff has made this statement on his broadcast on several occasions.

16. This movement involved famous Evangelical scholars and writers—men like A.J. Gordon, the scholarly Baptist pastor of Clarendon St. Baptist Church in Boston; A.B. Simpson, the Presbyterian who founded the Christian Missionary Alliance denomination; Andrew Murray, the Dutch Reformed pastor/devotional writer of South Africa; William Broadman of Boston, and others. Joe McIntyre, *E.W. Kenyon and His Message of Faith* (Bothell, WA: Empowering Grace, 2010) 46-48. For a better understanding of the relationship between healing and positive confession and its connection to the Holiness movement and other sources to positive confession, 53, 239-40, 245, 247, 249, 251, 253, 255, 257, 259-61, 263, 276, 284, 288, 296, 327, 348, 355.

17. Sweet has been called by some liberal apologists the first "scientific" historian of American Christianity. He became

dean at the divinity school of the University of Chicago
and attracted an excellent faculty of church historians
who wrote volumes of what became the accepted version
of American Protestant history. Sweet published the first
edition of his influential *The Story of Religion in America* in
1930, which continued to be reissued and reedited for thirty
years. In Sweet's vision, mainline Protestant Christianity
was the *Christianity of America*. He paid attention to the
fundamentalist versus liberal debates, church expansion, and
the missionary activities of the Protestant churches.

18. Paul King, *Only Believe*, 288-299; Nancy A. Hardesty, *Faith
Cure: Divine Healing in the Holiness and Pentecostal Movements*
(Peabody, MA: Hendrickson, 2003), 75-86.
Buckley was the editor of the most powerful Christian
newsletter of the day, the *Christian Advocate* of the Methodist
Episcopal Church. He fought against the Wesleyan theology
and experience and against the Faith Cure movement for
many years. DeArteaga writes, "Buckley battled the healing
revival all through the 1880s with his personally written lead
articles in the *Christian Advocate*. In 1886, his writings on
the subject were brought together, combined with his articles
on the cults and published as *Faith-Healing, Christian Science
and Kindred Phenomena*. A brief look at the table of contents
reveals his assumptions. All spiritual phenomena (ironically
including many of the experiences of John Wesley) were
lumped together as deviant and dangerous to the Christian's
life. Faith Cure was ranked with astrology and divination;
visions equated with witchcraft. Although he considered some
class of phenomena as natural, such as dreaming, even these
could be dangerous for the Christian if taken as spiritually
significant." DeArteaga, *Forging*, 220.

19. "Divine healing has been one of the most fascinating, yet
controversial themes to develop in the modern history and
theology of the American Church. It has also been one of
the few significant developments in the American Church,

which has remained almost completely unexamined by church historians. In fact, the existence of the Faith Cure movement was lost to church historians until the 1980s. It was only through a pioneer article in *Church History* by the Catholic historian Raymond Cunningham that the movement was rediscovered. The story of the Faith Cure movement has many tragedies. There was the tragedy of the mainline churches choosing consensus theology with its stealth heresy over the plain reading of Scripture versus the way of the Holy Spirit. The spirit of Phariseeism won. The greatest tragedy of all is that of missed opportunities for American Christendom. Christendom could have reaped a great harvest of healing, renewed Pentecost and power in prayer. Instead, a hailstorm of cessationism and the stealth heresy destroyed the crop just as it was ripening. Only gleanings were left for others to pick up." DeArteaga, *Forging*, 224-25.

20. King, *Only Believe*, chap. 20; Hardesty, *Faith Cure*, 75-86; Francis MacNutt, *The Healing Reawakening: Reclaiming Our Lost Inheritance* (Grand Rapids, MI: Chosen, 2006).

21. McIntyre, *E.W. Kenyon*, 60-93,

22. Historical Protestantism refers to the denominations of Protestantism up until the latter half of the nineteenth century with the birth of the Holiness denominations and the beginning of the twentieth century with the birth of the Pentecostal denominations. Historical Protestantism as used in the book does not include Holiness, Pentecostal, or Charismatic denominations or networks.

23. Nancy A. Hardesty, *Faith Cure*; Raymond Cunningham, "From Holiness to Healing: The Faith Cure in America, 1872-1892," *Church History* 43 (December 1974): 499-513.

24. Van A. Harvey, *The Historian and the Believer: The Morality of Historical Knowledge and Christian Belief* (New York, NY: MacMillan, 1969), 127-63, esp. chap. 5.

# CHAPTER THIRTEEN

1. The full story of this deliverance can be found in Friedrich Zündel, *The Awakening: One Man's Battle with Darkness* (Plough Publishing House, 2014), 1209-18, Kindle ebook.

2. Dispensationalism's primary exponents J.N. Darby and Edward Irving would develop a "working" relationship, but Darby, unlike Irving, would remain a cessationist. This relationship has been denied by Darbyites, but evidence can be found through the research of journalist Dave McPherson. Most historians have not recognized that Eduard Irving believed in the pre-tribulation rapture prior to J.N. Darby, neither do they recognize that Irving was influenced by a Jesuit priest who wrote as a "supposed" converted Jew. This Jesuit was trying to deal with the protestant commentators of the sixteenth century, the time he lived, seeing the Pope as the antichrist and the Catholic Church as the "great Whore of Babylon." Irving did not realize the book he was influenced by was written by a Catholic. Neither did J.N. Darby. This information is in the following dispensational articles that were not written by McPherson but by an anonymous writer called "a gospel preacher." This is one of the best resources I have ever found on dispensationalism. Dave McPherson, "Edward Irving is Unnerving," http://www.scionofzion.com/edward_irving.htm (accessed March 15, 2012); A Gospel Preacher, "The History of Dispensationalism," http://regal-network.com/dispensationalism/index.html (accessed March 15, 2012).

3. The Catholic Apostolic Church in London in the 1830s.

4. Clark and Johnson, *Essential Guide to Healing*, 105.

5. Brown, *Holy Laughter to Holy Fire*, 197-98.

6. Ibid.

7. Alma Bridwell White, *Demons and Tongues* (Eastfird, CT: Martino Publishing, 2013).

8. See Clark and Johnson, *Essential Guide to Healing*, 107-110.

9.   Ibid., 105-106.

10.  I have capitalized Charismatic in this book although most rules of grammar do not capitalize it. The reason I have done this is because, although there are no denominations in America that use the term *charismatic* as a proper noun, there are denominations in Mexico and other parts of the world that do. For this reason Charismatic and Pentecostal, when capitalized, refer to denominations and when in lower case are used as an adjective instead of a noun. It is time the rules of English caught up with the reality of the world's religious state! I have distinguished Pentecostals and Charismatics as another version of Christianity, along with the Catholics and Protestants, instead of including them as Protestants, following the lead of the President of Union Theological Seminary who, in the mid to late fifties, made this distinction. However, in Brazil all Christians are divided into only two categories—Catholics and Evangelicals—which is a very different use of the word *Evangelical* from the context of the United States.

11.  Ruthven, *On the Cessation*, 170.

12.  Francis MacNutt, *Healing* (Notre Dame, IN: Ave Maria Press, 1974), 31-32.

13.  Gregory Boyd, *God at War: The Bible and Spiritual Conflict* (Downers Grove, IL: InterVarsity Press, 1997). While indebted to Boyd for the language of warfare and blueprint worldviews, at this time I am not convinced of all of the conclusions Boyd draws from his warfare worldview—open theism. One does not have to adopt open theism to believe in a two-kingdom warfare worldview. There is disagreement among scholars on Boyd's attempted solution to the problem of evil. Catholic theologian Mary Healy writes:

> I think there is an important *partial* truth embedded in this description, but unfortunately it is presented in an exaggerated and theologically misguided way. Boyd's attempt at a solution to the problem of evil

departs from historic Christian doctrine as held by Protestants, Orthodox and Catholics. He denies or at least downplays God's omnipotence and omniscience (particularly God's knowledge of the future). He also makes light of the distinction between God's positive will and God's permissive will, which is crucial. Since God is all-good, he never directly wills evil. However, he does *permit* evil, because in His infinite wisdom and power He is able to bring a greater good out of it. To deny that God permits evil is to return to a kind of Manichean or polytheistic worldview in which God is not totally in control of the created universe. And this can ultimately contribute to despair in the face of evils that we do not successfully combat.

Boyd also misrepresents Augustine's teaching. For instance, on page eleven, he notes that "modern evangelical theology, following the Augustinian tradition, has tended to view angels merely as agents who invariably carry out God's sovereign will." However, this is not true. Both Augustine and modern evangelicals recognize the fact that there are fallen angels, (i.e., demons, which invariably resist God's sovereign will). Boyd has a significant insight regarding the emphasis of Christian teaching and the need to take seriously the biblical warfare worldview—but without compromising the omnipotence of God. It would be great if someone did a study of Augustine's views and their impact from a more balanced theological perspective.

Mary Healy, e-mail message to me, April 30, 2013, emphasis added.

14. Boyd, *God at War*, 10-27, esp. 21-22.

15. Dr. Mary Healey has also pointed out that this language and its understanding of *the Aquinas–Aristotelian synthesis* is misrepresentative of Aquinas who had so much to say about

the gifts of the Holy Spirit and belief in the supernatural realm. This language is from *Healing and Christianity* by Dr. Morton Kelsey.

16. Kelsey, *Healing and Christianity,* 203.

17. *Anointed by the Spirit,* 215, Kindle Ed.

18. Zündel, *The Awakening,* 1209-18.

## CHAPTER FOURTEEN

1. Ruthven states, "Accordingly, like the first-century popes, apostles wrote their encyclicals, too: the documents of the New Testament. It did not seem to occur to the Reformers that Scripture itself claims that only three of the 12, or 13, or 19, or 90 or more apostles (popes) actually wrote any part of the New Testament, and of that, only 45.8 percent by volume! Non-apostles wrote most of the New Testament! Oh well, let's not get picky about the Protestant idea of apostle." Ruthven, *What's Wrong,* 20.

2. Ruthven, *On the Cessation,* 189-206; "The two legs upon which Warfield built his argument both are broken. These two legs were his historical argument and his biblical argument." Ruthven, *What's Wrong,* 23.

3. "The Lord's hand was with them, and a great number of people believed and turned to the Lord" (Acts 11:21). The Lord's hand was an expression indicating the power of God was with them. And power in the New Testament foremost included the meaning of signs and wonders, miracles, and healing.

4. "Then Ananias went to the house and entered it. Placing his hands on Saul, he said, 'Brother Saul, the Lord—Jesus, who appeared to you on the road as you were coming here—has sent me so that you may see again and be filled with the Holy Spirit'" (Acts 9:17).

5. See Middleton, Conyers, *A Free Inquiry into the Miraculous Powers Which are Supposed to Have Subsisted in the Christian Church from the Earliest Ages thru Several Successive Centuries: By Which it is Shewn, that We have Not Sufficient Reason to Believe, Upon the Authority of the Primitive Fathers, that Any Such Powers Were Continued to the Church, After the Days of the Apostles* (London, UK: Manby and H.S. Cox, 1749); David Hume, *Enquiry Concerning Human Understanding*, 2nd ed. (Oxford, UK: Clarendon, 1902), especially his section, "On Miracles."

6. The arguments in this paragraph are dependent upon Ruthven (esp. Ruthven, *On the Cessation*). I read *On the Cessation of the Charismata* several years ago, developed three one-hour lectures out of his book, and developed extensive chapters from Ruthven in the author's workbook, Clark, *Empowered*, 125-60. Having taught this material scores of times, the arguments have become so internalized that there might be language that is not cited due to this internalization. Suffice to say, this subject is heavily drawn from Ruthven's arguments.

7. Ruthven, *On the Cessation*. Warfield's concept of miracle is refuted on pages 57-82, his historical argument is refuted on pages 82-92, his biblical hermeneutic is refuted on pages 93-110, his polemic on post-biblical miracles is refuted due to his inadequate understanding of the Holy Spirit and the Kingdom of God on pages 111-23.

## CHAPTER FIFTEEN

1. Jack Deere, *Surprised by the Voice of God* (Grand Rapids, MI: Zondervan Publishing House, 1998), 64-79. Deere, *Surprised by the Power*, especially appendix B and C, 229-67.

2. Mary Crawford, *The Shantung Revival: The Greatest Revival in Baptist Church History* (Mechanicsburg, PA: Global Awakening, 2005). This is the original version republished by Global Awakening with a short afterward pointing out the

similar phenomena of the Shantung Revival and that of the Toronto Blessing.

3.   Tongues occurred during the Second Great Awakening at a revival, which touched students from the University of Georgia. Vinson Synan, *The Holiness-Pentecostal Movement in the United States* (Grand Rapids, Michigan, Wm. B. Eerdmans Pub. Co., 1971), 24-25.

4.   Vinson Synan, "Lecture on Revival."

5.   Vinson Synan, *In the Latter Days: The Outpouring of the Holy Spirit in the Twentieth Century*, revised edition (Fairfax, VA: Xulon Press, 2001), passim. This is a great read of how the revival spread from the Los Angeles to the world. However, this would not be entirely true because God was also breaking out in India, Chile, and Korea during this time.

6.   Brown, *Testing Prayer*, 66; Lederle, *Theology with Spirit*, 60.

7.   I graduated December 1977 and do not know if this has been rectified or not.

8.   At least in my four years of religious studies in college and three years in seminary, including the special class on revival taught by Dr. Lewis Drummond, the Pentecostal revivals were not mentioned.

9.   I was educated at Oakland City University, a Baptist University, BS degree in Religious Studies 1974; The Southern Baptist Theological Seminary, MDiv degree, and United Theological Seminary 1977; and DMin degree granted December 2012, United Theological Seminary. I was an ordained Baptist minister from 1972 to 1984. During this time I often read sermons by Spurgeon, owning his entire sermon collection of many volumes. Around 1983-1984 I read in a couple of Spurgeon's sermons where he stopped and gave a word of knowledge about personal details of persons in the congregation. I do not know which sermon I was reading, and time did not allow me to research it. The index does not have a category "words of knowledge."

10. Russell H. Conwell, *Life of Charles Haddon Spurgeon The World's Greatest Preacher* (Philadelphia, PA: Edgewood Publishing Co., 1892), Chapter 7 "Wonderful Healing." Russell H. Conwell, "Preaching Prayer and Compassion," Healing and Revival.com, Healing and Revival Press, http://healingandrevival.com/BioCHSpurgeon.htm (accessed July 2, 2014).

11. Vinson Synan, *In the Latter Days: The Outpouring of the Holy Spirit in the Twentieth Century* (Fairfax, VA: Xulon Press, 2001), 31. Randy Clark, Sch*ool of Healing and Impartation Workbook: Spiritual and Medical Perspectives* (Mechanicsburg, PA: Global Awakening, 2008), 5. Spurgeon's prophesy was:

> Another great work of the Holy Spirit, which is not accomplished, is the bringing on of the latter-day glory. In a few more years—I know not when, I know not how—the Holy Spirit will be poured out in far different style from the present. There are diversities of operations; and during the last few years it has been the case that the diversified operations have consisted of very little pouring out of the Spirit. Ministers have gone on in dull routine, continually preaching—preaching—preaching, and little good has been done. I do hope that a fresh era has dawned upon us, and that there is a better pouring out of the Spirit even now. For the hour is coming, and it may be even now, when the Holy Ghost will be poured out again in such a wonderful manner, that many will run to and from and knowledge shall be increased—the knowledge of the Lord shall cover the earth as the waters cover the surface of the great deep; when His Kingdom shall come, and His will shall be done on earth as it is in heaven....my eyes flash with the thought that very likely I shall live to see the out-pouring of the Spirit; when "the sons and the daughters of God shall

prophesy, and the young men shall see visions, and the old men shall dream dreams."

12. A.J. Gordon (Baptist), A.B. Simpson (Presbyterian and who would later become the founder of the Christian Missionary Alliance), Andrew Murray (Dutch Reformed South Africa), and others from the Reformed theological tradition.

13. Hardesty, *Faith Cure.*

14. Gustaf Aulen, *Christus Victor: An Historical Study of the Three Main Types of the Idea of Atonement*, trans. H.G. Herbert (New York, NY: MacMillan Publishing Co., 1969), 20.

15. Leon Morris, *The Cross in the New Testament* (Grand Rapids, MI: Wm. B. Eerdmans Publishers, 1999). This is an excellent work on the understanding of the atonement with a special emphasis upon the substitutionary atonement viewpoint.

16. Frank Bartleman, *Azusa Street* (New Kensington, PA: Whitaker House, 1982).

17. Synan, *The Holiness-Pentecostal Movement*, 53, 163. A few years earlier there had been twenty-three new Holiness denominations founded between 1893–1900.

18. Hardesty, *Faith Cure*, 139-42, especially 140.

19. Hardesty, *Faith Cure*, 87-99.

20. Billy Graham, *Just As I Am* (New York, NY: Harper, 1997) 163-64.

21. Letter from Stephen Olford, May 9, 1996. Cf. Marshall Frady, *Billy Graham* (Boston: Little, Brown, 1979); *William Martin, A Prophet with Honor* (New York: William Morrow, 1991). John Pollock, Billy Graham (London: Hodder & Stoughton, 1966), 62, http://www.ccel.us/billy.ch1.html (accessed July 2015).

22. Randy Clark, *There Is More: Reclaiming the Power of Impartation*, First Edition (Mechanicsburg, PA: Global Awakening, 2006).

# CONCLUSION

1.  Clark, *There Is More*, 91-104. During this same time Dr. Francis MacNutt was writing a book on the same subject that was very similar to material in *There Is More* and even more similar to materials in my workbook for the *School of Healing and Impartation: Empowered.* Cf. Francis MacNutt, *The Nearly Perfect Crime: How the Church Almost Killed the Ministry of Healing* (Grand Rapids, MI: Chosen, 2005). This book has been renamed in a later version, *The Healing Reawakening: Reclaiming Our Lost Inheritance.*

2.  Clark, *Healing River,* 3, 19.

3.  Clark, *Healing River,* 109.

# INDEX

# ABOUT RANDY CLARK

Randy Clark, with a D.Min. from United Theological Seminary, is the founder of Global Awakening, a teaching, healing, and impartation ministry that crosses denominational lines. An in-demand international speaker, he leads the Apostolic Network of Global Awakening and travels extensively for conferences, international missions, leadership training, and humanitarian aid. Randy and his wife, DeAnne, live in Pennsylvania.

# WATCH GOD ACCOMPLISH THE MIRACULOUS

# THROUGH YOU.

## LEARN FROM DR. RANDY CLARK!

Every Christian has been sent and empowered by Jesus to heal the sick. The problem is that many of us don't know how to practically complete this task.

In the *Power to Heal* curriculum, international evangelist, teacher, and apostolic voice, Dr. Randy Clark, shares eight practical, Bible-based tools that will help you start praying for the sick and see them supernaturally healed!

# THE HOLY SPIRIT
## WANTS TO WORK THROUGH YOU!

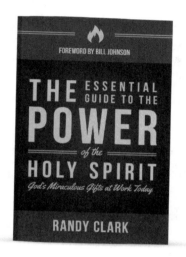

## MANY CHRISTIANS HAVE EMBRACED THE DECEPTION THAT THE HOLY SPIRIT IS NO LONGER AT WORK.

But Dr. Randy Clark, President and Founder of Global Awakening, has been an *eyewitness* to the miraculous work of the Holy Spirit and a *key participant* in watching Him powerfully transform lives throughout the world. In this easy-to-read guide, he equips believers to understand and walk in the power of the Spirit every day.

- Discover the gifts of the Holy Spirit that are available to you.
- Recognize an authentic move of God in your church, community, & life.
- Understand how miracles, signs, and wonders play a key role evangelism.

## FULFILL YOUR DESTINY! UNLOCK THE POWER OF THE HOLY SPIRIT IN YOUR LIFE.

 Destiny Image is a division of Nori Media Group.

**globalawakening**

lighting fires • building bridges • casting vision

Based in Mechanicsburg, PA, the Apostolic Network of Global Awakening (ANGA) is a teaching, healing and impartation ministry with a heart for the nations. Founded in 1994 by Randy Clark after his involvement with the Toronto Airport Christian Fellowship revival, the ministry exists to fulfill the biblical commissions of Jesus:

*As you go preach, saying the Kingdom of heaven is at hand. Heal the sick, cleanse the lepers, raise the dead, cast out demons. Freely you have received, freely give (Matthew 10:7-8).*

*Therefore go and make disciples of all nations, baptizing them in the name of the Father and of the Son and of the Holy Spirit, and teaching them to obey everything I have commanded you. And surely I am with you always, to the very end of the age (Matthew 28:19-20).*

Through the formation of ANGA, International Ministry Trips (IMT), the Schools of Healing and Impartation and the Global School of Supernatural Ministry, Global Awakening offers training, conferences, humanitarian aid, and ministry trips in an effort to raise up a company of men and women who will facilitate revival among the nation's leaders. By providing an assortment of international training opportunities, the ministry works in accordance with the revelation to the Apostle Paul regarding the purpose of the five fold ministries:

*It was He who gave some to be apostles, some to be prophets, some to be evangelists, and some to be pastors and teachers, to prepare God's people for works of service, so that the body of Christ may be built up until we all reach unity in the faith and in the knowledge of the Son of God and become mature, attaining to the whole measure of the fullness of Christ (Ephesians 4:11-13).*

Led by Rev. Randy Clark, the ministry has visited over 36 countries and continues to travel extensively to bring hope, healing, and power to the nations.

**globalawakening.com**

## Christian Prophetic
### CERTIFICATION PROGRAM

We are happy to announce the launch of the
**Christian Prophetic Certification Program
(CPCP).**

CPCP will teach students how to recognize the gift of prophecy in their own life, allowing them to better recognize communications from the Holy Spirit.

Students will gain a truly Biblical perspective on the prophetic both from the Old and New Testaments. They will also learn about the history of prophesy within the church, its benefits and the ways in which it went off track.

**Courses are available online
and can be taken anywhere at any time.**

Check out our website for more details at
**propheticcertification.com**

**JOIN US!**

# FREE E-BOOKS?
## YES, PLEASE!

Get **FREE** and deeply-discounted **Christian books** for your **e-reader** delivered to your inbox **every week!**

## IT'S SIMPLE!

**VISIT** lovetoreadclub.com

**SUBSCRIBE** by entering your email address

**RECEIVE** free and discounted e-book offers and inspiring articles delivered to your inbox every week!

Unsubscribe at any time.

# SUBSCRIBE NOW!

> ## LOVE TO READ CLUB

visit **LOVETOREADCLUB.COM** ▶